DIARY OF A GERMAN SOLDIER

WILHELM PRÜLLER

DIARY OF A GERMAN SOLDIER

Edited by H. C. Robbins Landon
and Sebastian Leitner

With an Introduction by
Robert Leckie

COWARD-McCANN, INC.
NEW YORK

FIRST AMERICAN EDITION, 1963

English translation by
H. C. Robbins Landon

Library of Congress Catalog
Card Number: 63-20759

MANUFACTURED IN THE UNITED STATES OF AMERICA

CONTENTS

INTRODUCTION
by Robert Leckie

Within the memory of a middle-aged man the German nation has twice hurled itself upon combinations of the most powerful nations on earth and has twice come within grasp of victory. In the second attempt under Adolf Hitler, Nazi Germany not only ranged farther in conquest and came closer to ultimate victory than did the Imperial Germany of Kaiser Wilhelm, but also unleashed upon the world a bestiality calculated to make even the Kaiser's tarnished spurs shine forth in chivalrous brilliance.

How did this happen, we ask ourselves—and why was it so?

Some of the answers might be found in this book. This is not to suggest that in *Diary of a German Soldier* we are going to find the German caricature of our own propaganda—the strutting, swinish, sadistic, slavish Teuton—but rather that here we may discover exactly those human features which, in the abusive service of the Nazi beast, became inhuman.

Here is the diary of Wilhelm Prüller, a born writer, able to set down with compelling clarity all those experiences which were his after he crossed the Polish frontier on the first day of the war to serve, thereafter, in the Battle for France, the war in the Balkans, and, finally, in Russia from the invasion to the bitter bloody end. Here is also a young conscript from Vienna who is an ardent and believing Nazi. As such, he gives us a measure of how completely the Nazi shibboleths had captured the minds and hearts of Hitler's most ordinary followers. It is as though people such as Wilhelm Prüller were looking for Nazism before it came along, as though if it had not happened by, they would have invented it. All its brutalities and boasting are joys to Prüller's heart.

In his diary he parrots *Der Führer*'s speeches, he gives direful lectures to Churchill and Daladier, he threatens errant non-Nazi nations with fiery retribution, he grinds "inferior peoples" into the dust beneath his feet, and he mends the broken hearts of war widows with the goo of superpatriotism. In the end, when the armies of the "inferior peoples" are tearing the German Wehrmacht apart, he continues to play the broken record of racial superiority. He is like a man going down under his enemy's charge shouting, "I've got you!"

Yet, automatic Nazi that he may be, Wilhelm Prüller is also an excellent soldier. He seems as typical for the German Wehrmacht as the cartoonist Bill Mauldin's Willie and Joe were typical of the U. S. Armed Forces.

And he is so different.

Here is the attraction of this book. Wilhelm Prüller is not a bit like G.I. Joe. True enough, he feels all the emotions of war in the same way, he suffers in the same way. Anyone who has been in battle can share the dryness of his throat as he lies in a ditch watching the approach of a monster Russian tank. But Prüller neither thinks nor acts the same way.

Chief of all, Wilhelm Prüller and most of his *kameradan* are serious. Prüller hymns *Der Führer, Volk und Vaterland* so often in his diary that it would make the lighthearted American dog-face blush to read it. Prüller himself would be enraged to hear the raggedy-tailed Marine translate his Corps' watchword, *Semper Fidelis* or "Always Faithful," into the sardonic "I-got-mine-how'd-you-make-out?" Therein lies the difference. Though conscripts, Prüller and his comrades think like professionals. More, they have a purpose. They believe in the glorious destiny of Germany—in this case Nazi Germany—and are willing to sacrifice for it. They even accept death as a fact of soldierly life. Such purpose, especially when it is deluded and led by an ideological aberration, has often been described as "blind fanaticism." Unfortunately, an American who sees it lunging at him behind a bayonet is unable to disqualify it with an epithet.

Military professionalism, when yoked to romantic purpose, however evil, is a most formidable force. With one eye on certain new enemies of ours, we might take counsel from this diary: we might discover how what is best in man can be brought to excellence in the service of what is worst.

1. THE POLISH CAMPAIGN

30th August 1939

In this diary I shall attempt to describe to you, my dearly beloved Henny, all the things that happen to me and my unit. I will also tell you those things about me that you ought to know.

Personally, I think the 'Affaire Poland' will be settled peacefully: perhaps Daladier will at the last minute assume the function of a mediator. But if it really does come to war, I am sure it won't last long. For the Poles won't be able to withstand our attack.

And how could England and France fulfil their promise to help Poland? The West Wall is impregnable. France would sacrifice her sons there to no avail. And England could only rush to help Poland by sea. The Baltic has certainly been closed by us. Gibraltar will be held at bay by Italy and Spain. The only people who could help the Poles are the Soviet Union. And a brilliant stroke of strategy has destroyed this Polish hope, too.

Perhaps the Soviet Union will send an ultimatum to Poland and demand their centuries-old rights.

No matter. The situation is highly satisfactory for us, and it's unthinkable for us, too, as the greatest European power, to sit back and watch the persecution of the Volksdeutsche without doing something. It is our duty to rectify this wrong, which cries to Heaven. If we fight, then we know that we are serving a rightful cause. We know, however, that the Führer will do all he can to avoid war.

1st September 1939

It's 4 a.m. We are 2 miles from the border and ready to go.

The Poles haven't accepted our rightful demands.

At 5.45 a.m. the border is supposed to be crossed.

We're a reserve unit. One hundred metres at our side there is a large oil, petroleum or armaments factory. One grenade . . . and we've had it.

We're sitting on our lorries and telling dirty jokes. Everything is camouflaged.

Only a quarter of an hour more. If only this waiting were over. If only something would happen. One way or the other.

For a week they put us up on the bare floor of a school. Waiting, waiting. We haven't slept for nights. And the worst of it is, you're not allowed to write home. Terrible. We're not to write till 4th September.

We've just got paid. One hundred Czech crowns. A joke. In two hours we may not even be in this world. And with 100 crowns in our pockets. And not able to send a last message home, while our dear ones are waiting for news.

One's thoughts go in a circle—as if they wanted to turn a huge mill-stone. Everything on edge. And the feeling that we're in this place: painful when you think of home. The most wonderful feeling as well, though, of manly and loyal devotion to duty!

My darling Henny! I don't know how long it'll last. I want to tell you something lovely: you were the only woman I've ever loved. And if God pleases that I return home, then I know one thing: as long as I live, you'll be the only woman I'll ever love. Before I saw you—yes, there were others, but it wasn't love. You taught that to me. I could start at the Bürgerball, I could talk of your first holiday, of my departure to Berlin and my return. I could recall our marriage, my call-up . . . it wouldn't be complete, though, if I didn't think of our Lore. Guard her well, this little creature. Make her strong, so that one day she can skirt the cliffs of life. And tell her, sometimes, of me, if it should happen that. . . .

You both are my hope in this and the coming hours.

And send my best greetings to your mother. She was an idol to me, this wonderful woman. And to my parents, especially my father. And to anyone else who would like to have them. Of course your father, too.

Something else for you: keep on being the wife you always were, be assured that I love only you, and that I live only for you. I don't ask anything from you. Only that you should think of me often, and know that in my life I've only done my duty, nothing but my duty. And stay happy, even in the misfortune of my death.

6.20: the first news: our troops have pushed 3 miles into Poland. The first village has been taken. No shot from the Polish side.

6.45: we move forward.

7.30: the Poles tried a tank attack. They were destroyed and forced to run. While retreating they set fire to six villages.

Our own unit is on our side of the border, although some of our troops are 6 km. into Poland. It's begun to rain now. I've wrapped my MG in a woollen blanket; this might save our lives. To the right are the Tatra Mountains and in front of us a burning village.

We've reached the border.

It is a wonderful feeling, now, to be a German.

Flak pushes past us—artillery, tanks and armoured scouting cars, hundreds of them.

We're still on the border. The row of tanks has no end. A quarter of an hour, tanks, tanks, tanks. . . . Rain's stopped. The crew of our lorry is all tense. Seven men and a noncom, we all wish we were in Poland. . . .

9 o'clock: moving forward at a walking pace. Forward a few feet, then waiting, waiting. . . . Just learned that we've occupied Danzig.

9.45: We've crossed the border. We're in Poland. *Deutschland, Deutschland über alles!*

We're 103 km. from Krakow. Everywhere we see torn-up roads, trenches, tank traps hastily thrown up. Destroyed bridges make us take long detours across fields. We drive through the first village. They hand flowers into our lorry. In delight they stretch their hands towards us. The blown-up bridges and the torn-up streets continue to slow up our advance. But all the Poles' efforts are shown to be of no avail. The German Wehrmacht is marching! If we look back, or in front of us, or left or right: everywhere the motorized Wehrmacht!

Suddenly, halt! Enemy in front of us. I've got to take my machine-gun section and act as a scouting patrol. About a mile up the hill. Ha! . . . we're shot at from the right. The first time! Machine-gun volley, it doesn't reach us. Then silence. Our lorry climbs the hill. We go back to the Squadron, and leave the lorries.

We march to the attack. Terrific heat now. Battledress. The machine-gun 13½ kg. on our backs. One mile, two, three, on, on. . . . We can't go on. But mile after mile is captured. No one can go on. No water, no coffee, no tea. Marching, running, running. Halt! We've reached a PAK (anti-tank gun) and rest in front of a few houses. The family sits in front of the door. All of them crying. But we aren't harming anyone! Why didn't the Polish Government give in? We haven't got anything against the people themselves. But where are our rights? They offer us water and milk. We refuse, because we have to. But this thirst is terrible!

Our artillery begins to fire again. At every shot the Poles wince. Under the shell-fire we march on. It's 16.45. We've marched only 3 hours and have 10 km. behind us. I hope we stay here. A hamlet. But there's supposed to be a pub: then we'd have something to drink. Blank goes past and has already got a bottle of beer. It's the last. He chucks it at me. Undrinkable. As if it were warmed up.

It's now 17.30. I am so tired I could drop. My feet ache. I've been on my feet since 1 in the morning. One thing kept me going today, the thought of our seeing each other again. I'm still alive, and so are you and Lore. All of us!

2nd September 1939

Yesterday evening at 9 was the end. We slept in an open field at night. Supper was pork soup and tea. I was so tired that I slept at once. Then: our troop had to get up and act as a patrol. Somewhere there's shooting. We're supposed to find out what it's all about. For one and a half hours we scour the countryside. Nothing. I think it must have been the civilian population in action. At 1 o'clock I was able to sleep again. At 5 in the morning we get up, and the march goes on. On foot. We can't use the lorries because the enemy is expected.

7.30: we rest. No water, nothing to drink, nothing to wash in. Cigarettes are finished, and of course we can't buy any. Perhaps we can grab some tomorrow. At 3.00 in the morning our artillery began to fire, and for 4 whole hours they roared away.

14.00: we've climbed a big hill. Hours it took. In front of us the guns boom, also light machine-gun fire. For the past hours they've been under fire from our artillery and trench mortars, but they wouldn't give in.

We're lying ready in a wood. Banging of rifle shots. We learn that there are five civilians behind our back shooting at us. I go with two others, and in a few minutes these five civilians have had it.

14.30: the first Polish reconnaissance aircraft. He shot a few rounds at us and disappeared. Our flak saw him, shot at him, and, I hope, got him. The Poles seem to be well entrenched, but our artillery clears the way for us. Over hills and valleys, through burning villages we continue to attack. We take some civilians with us, and they have to carry our heavy things. The guns still boom. 5.00: our first soldier killed, from the 7th Squadron. We march on, the fight continues. Today we packed it up early. We lay on the ground. Naturally. No food till 11.30 p.m. Tea and cigarettes! 15! Then sleep, sleep. Today I'm still alive, and so are you and Lore! All of us!

3rd September 1939

At 6.00 we get up, more tired than the day before. Today, our first wedding anniversary! How can we celebrate it? I: in the woods, ready to attack. You: thinking of me, not knowing where I am. Sad, isn't it? But there's nothing to do about it, is there? It's war! Just what is war? A compilation of sacrifices and exhaustion, of thirst and occasionally hunger, of heat and cold. I hope it's finished soon.

In my thoughts I'm back a year ago. And I think, and think . . . I hope the attack ends well for me.

The attack has been cancelled: what's happening?

11.00: The Führer is said to have issued an ultimatum to the Poles, that they should give us the land we've taken. If there's no satisfactory answer by 12.00, 2,000 of our planes will take off at 12.01 and destroy cities and villages. That would mean practically the end of Poland. The Poles ought to accept.

11.15: plenty of excitement. Polish flyers appear and shoot at us, the flak goes into action. One, two, three they are all shot down. At 11.30 we prepare to march towards Krakow. It's supposed to be a forced march. Perhaps in connection with the ultimatum. Perhaps Poland is already done for today.[1]

We've taken a pig with us. Devil of a job to load her. Perhaps we'll eat her in Krakow. 12.45: departure. At 13.00 five Polish planes attack: 3 are shot down. 13.30: shots at us from the woods. Half an hour's wait. At 18.00, demount and prepare for battle. I don't really think that there'll be a fight today. We'll probably remain in position and attack tomorrow morning.

We've heard a piece of news. If the war isn't over by midnight, Russia and Latvia will attack. That would be a decisive move. The attack is called off. I've not eaten or drunk anything since this morning. But I'm still alive today, and so are you and Lore. All of us!

4th September 1939

Following night patrol, we proceed at 5.00 towards Krakow. Yesterday some of us were killed, and many wounded. Enemy artillery fires against us. We destroy it. Altogether, I've a great deal of faith in our weapons. Yesterday the Poles were ready for

[1] The original German text 'Vielleicht ist Polen heute schon verloren' is a sarcastic rewording of a line from the Polish National Hymn 'Noch ist Polen nicht verloren' ('Poland is not yet lost . . .')

battle for the umpteenth time. They continue to withdraw. They should face and fight us in a decent and manly way. But not a bit of it!

Our road to Krakow is marked by burning villages, which were set on fire by the artillery, or by us if we encountered any resistance. Yesterday evening the whole countryside was red with fire.

7.00 in the morning: we haven't had anything to eat since yesterday at 2.30 a.m. Our usual meal consists of black coffee for breakfast, tea and something warm for supper. But you can keep going on that, because now and then Schmalz (fat) or Leverwurst turns up, and during the day we feed ourselves on beets, fruit and so on. 9.15: finally we get coffee. How good that tasted!

12.30–1 o'clock: momentous fight with Polish machine-gun emplacement very solidly entrenched. At last we were able to chuck them out. Stuparits and I went up forward right to the line, but the munition boys couldn't get to us. It was tough. But we came through it. At 7.00 p.m. we are told that we're to go somewhere else. Our orders are now completed. Three divisions have met. The road to Krakow is open, and we're 35 miles away. But we're still moving. Where to? We left at 20.00. Only four days of war! But full of danger and wonderful experiences! Today I'm still alive, and so are you and Lore. All of us!

5th September 1939

We didn't get very far yesterday. Either there were too many troop transports on the road or we hadn't had our orders yet. We pushed on for only half an hour and then stayed the whole night with our lorries on the road. After midnight, heavy artillery went past us all the time towards the heart of Poland. The road almost shook. This morning I had a real bath again. Although it's as cold at night as in the middle of winter, today is a marvellous day.

Markl slaughtered a pig, cooked and roasted it, made some plum sauce, and then we sat around, eating it; but our thoughts are at home just the same. When will we have our first meal at home again?

Oh, yes, I forgot to tell you: yesterday afternoon we really lived it up: chickens, geese, pigs, rabbits were killed and roasted on a wooden pole like a spit, and we gobbled them up at a great rate. But we had to move on in the evening.

11.30: we move on. It's said that the Russians have marched into Poland. I think the war will be over in a fortnight. Today we were issued cigarettes—14 and 4 cigars! Today we move towards Dobrawa. On the 3rd, after the attack had been called off, we saw a Polish PAK, a Polish tank and a motor-cycle with the driver, all shot by our PAKs. The motor-cycle driver looked dreadful. Today we went past again. On the roadside a little mound, a simple cross and flowers. One of the Poles lies buried here. He did his duty.

We drive the whole night. During the night we heard two more rumours: (1) that the English are supposed to have bombed Cologne and Königsberg; (2) that one of our Red-Cross columns is supposed to have been attacked by the Poles. Everyone killed. If it's true, and I meet a Pole, whoever he is, he's had it. To kill helpless, wounded and broken men, who according to international law mustn't be hurt! Nothing could be more barbarous. Today I'm still alive, and so are you and Lore!

6th September 1939

At 4.00 a.m. we moved on; first we went back to Rabka and now eastwards. Towards Lemberg. The night was cold, but short. We spent it in our vehicles. I think that we'll be allowed to write letters today. Maybe then I'll lie down on the grass to write to my beloved wife. . . .

12.00: we stop. We are fired at. We just went through Neu-Sandec. A smallish town which was still in Polish hands tonight. Here in Lipniza there was a Polish family, complete with goods and chattels. When they saw that no one intended to harm them, they wanted to give us lots of chocolate. We thank them and refuse, help them on their way, and give them good advice. The people are overjoyed and are certainly sure that no German is a barbarian.

The squad that shot at us is taken prisoner. Later we take 6 more prisoners, who surrendered. They tell us that they haven't eaten for three days. And that their people, whom we're pursuing, have been gone for eight hours. Altogether it seems to me, in all the days, that the Polish army flees in haste and leaves only a few men behind, who are supposed to hinder us by firing a few shots at us. Which they succeed in doing a hundred per cent. Since dawn we have been in Galicia, the hotly contested land of the year 1914.

14.00 to 16.00 hours: exchange of fire with Polish MGs and PAKs. Many prisoners, many fled. Fifty kilometres to our goal, Tarnow. We follow the fleeing Poles, and corner them on the next hill. We shoot madly. As we are about to storm the hill, a Pole comes at us with a white cloth. He surrenders. All the rest have gone already. It turns out that he's a Volksdeutscher. He shows us his gun: he didn't shoot at us. He should have. What a fate! A German, having to shoot at Germans. For the time being he gets into our lorry.

In the evening the trip continues. We have to go through several villages, and we have to be prepared for the fact that the Poles who fled will shoot at us as we go through. We drive about 30 km., the whole detachment at once. I drive with my group in the 3rd vehicle. One village, two, three, nothing happens.

23.30: all at once a rain of bullets descends on us. Drivers and the others jump off and run for the ditches. We stay put. Shots, shots. The two front vehicles have crossed a bridge—shells, MG fire, small arms . . . for ten minutes the bullets whistle over and past us. Then—at last our side opens fire. It sounds like salvation. Two hundred vehicles behind us, full of Kameraden, and all of them shooting. Fifteen minutes. Then a short pause. I grab my MG and with one leap I'm in the ditch, shooting like mad. I don't think the whole Polish army could have captured my car.

It's a long time before the firing subsides. Then I feel my way back to the troops. I have to take over security for the rest of the night. For a long time the Poles continue to shoot back, sporadically. Till morning. . . . It was the most creepy feeling, today, because you have to consider that we knew from prisoners that we'd be attacked if we travelled at night. And despite this . . . I had already said farewell to this world, but I was protected by you, darling Henny, by the flowers from your wedding bouquet, or by the pictures, or the letters I have with me. At any rate, I'm still alive today, and so are you and Lore. All of us!

7th September 1939

Today, at last, we've been put back in reserve again. We're spending the morning cleaning our weapons and having baths. Today the news reaches us by our radio transmitter car that Krakow has been taken. Could it be true? I wanted to write to you now, but we've got to push on. Towards Tarnow (10 o'clock).

At 12.00 we stop. I and my MG squad are called to go forward. Report to Squadron HQ, report to Battalion HQ, then to Regimental HQ,[1] where our Deputy Squadron Commander is waiting for us. We've been chosen as advance patrol for the Division. We are to find out where the enemy has withdrawn to, etc. Twelve km. in advance of the lines are to be reconnoitred. The return, and the moving back and forwards across the country, add up to some 30 km. And we've not yet eaten. Tarnow is to be taken tomorrow morning. Anyway, we've had a very worthwhile job entrusted to us.

It was awful. We combed about 20 km. but on the whole didn't find much. The main part of the enemy forces has withdrawn. We wanted to find out what roads he was taking, and in which direction he was running. We come within 10 metres of the road. Stuparits goes ahead to observe the convoy which is passing along the road. He comes running back, out of breath. It's the Poles! They're going northwards, so as to follow the map and then go towards east or west. If they turn off to the west,

[1] It will be remembered that the German army's cavalry units consisted of *Schwadron*, *Abteilung*, *Regiment*, which we have translated as Squadron, Battalion and Regiment(al).

they'll run smack into our advancing 1st Battalion of the Rifle Regiment. That'd be frightful. We must find out where the Poles will turn to. Up the hill. Lieutenant Wackermann suggests we go once again and find out for sure if it really is Poles who are marching on the road. We creep along the ditches. The vehicles roar past. No lights. Dust, dust. They can't be recognized. Then we hear in the distance a motor-cycle coming. We decide to stop it. If it's a Pole, we'll shoot him down, and if it's one of us, that's fine. The motor-cycle comes. But there are three of them. One of us stands on the road and waves with a red light. They stop. We rush at them with pistols and rifles. They're Germans!

Our task is accomplished. We've got to get the news to the Division. How shall we get there quickly? We stop vehicle after vehicle. Finally we get a ride from an engineering unit of the 9th Reconnaissance Rgt. They have enormously high trucks, full of gear. We drive without lights, of course. Stuparits and I on one of the trucks, the others on other ones. Look out! The truck's keeling over towards my side . . . it goes over the bank and falls down ten metres. I crawl out of the mess. My feet are giving me hell. Where's Stuparits? I shout. 'Here, here.' I drag away everything lying on top of him, undo his belt, open his coat. He seems to have broken some of his ribs. I can barely walk myself. I seem to have twisted both my ankles. At 3 o'clock in the morning we reach the Division and at 4.30 our Squadron. Hungry, thirsty, sleepy . . . and how cold it is! I'm still alive today, and so are you and Lore. All of us!

8th September 1939

We're standing on the road and putting our things in order. Tarnow was taken in the night. What next?

The Polish Government is supposed to have fled to Finland. Krakow, Bromberg, Graudenz and I don't know what else are in German hands. I wrote you today. Not much, but I didn't have time for more.

At noon we leave. Through Pilcno, Debica. I don't know where we are going. *En route* we meet numerous prisoners, see vehicles shot to pieces, guns, soldiers and masses of ammunition of all kinds. We're travelling towards Rzeszow. At almost every crossroads we come upon soldiers and horses laid out flat by our bombers. A whole company of Poles passes us going the other way: prisoners. Somewhere along the road we stop and spend the night in our vehicles. I must give up my MG and become Troop Leader, because Stuparits is lying in the hospital with broken ribs. Today I'm alive, and so are you and Lore. All of us!

10th September 1939

We're moving at a terrific pace. The roads are simply beyond description. And the Polish dead every foot. The dust is at least a foot deep. Our truck has something wrong with it. The Squadron moves on. When we get our truck going again, we hunt in vain for the Squadron for four hours.

Our driver's mate, Hofer, again proved to be idiocy personified. We go through a large town, which our bombers had flattened out yesterday. Hours ago, our Detachment took 1,000 prisoners here. Thousands of refugees. Civilians. We move through the town. On the railway embankment you can still see Polish soldiers fleeing in the direction of Przemysl. For protection's sake our observers and MGs are set up on the embankment. In a wagon in front of us an MG is mounted. Hofer still wants to go off towards Przemysl. At first they wouldn't let him through. He finally did get through, but after about 5 miles he sees it won't do us any good to go on like this. Finally he turns round.

A few hours ago our soldiers went through, but Hofer goes right up to some Polish civilians and asks after our unit. An idiot! Finally he takes my advice and asks after the regimental staff, which we'd seen somewhere along the way. There we learn that our unit hasn't arrived yet but it is due to pass through. That's cost us three hours in the thick of the dust.

We're thirsty and want to wash. We go into a house and get milk which we saw being milked from the cow in front of our eyes. Marvellous! The woman hasn't any bread. We give her some of ours, we've more than we need. She doesn't want to take it, for the Poles and the Jews have pretended to these simple people that the provisions and snacks we distribute are poisoned. We have to eat the bread in front of her, then she's satisfied.

I just learn that Göring spoke at 1 p.m. yesterday. He is supposed to have said that the war will be over in three or four days.

At 4 p.m. our Squadron arrives. We join it and drive to the next village. Some trains with refugees and military have arrived at Radymno. The soldiers have holed up in the goods wagons and are firing at us. We've already collected 20 wounded. Then our flyers arrive, they do their job on the trains and the railway embankment. Everyone rushes out of the cars into our hands.

We're thoroughly proud of our planes. I think that the most beautiful feelings a person can have are love and pride. And I place both of these on the same level, that's for certain. For if you are proud of something, then you have to love it. You can't be proud of a thing, a person, an animal, etc., unless you love it. And we love our Luftwaffe and are proud of it.

Today I'm still alive, and so are you and Lore! All of us!

11th September 1939

In the early hours a Polish reconnaissance plane appears, but it is so high that it can't be reached by our flak. We're still lying in the field. I sleep. And I had the following silly dream:

The war is taking place near Vienna. In Mauer. At noon I go to you and want to take you with me, to show you everything.[1]

Then I'm awakened: one hundred metres in front of me a Polish reconnaissance plane is flying, at the most he's 50 metres up. I grab my gun and pump 1, 2, 4, 5 shots into him. To no avail. Then two German pursuit planes arrive, chase him, and in a few minutes he's done for.

At 4.00 we're taken off and moved to another position. Naturally we dig in again. Jaroslaw was taken today. The enemy

[1] Prüller's dream came true, in so far as the Russians took Mauer (a suburb of Vienna) in 1945. Prüller was not there at the time, as will be seen. (*See below*, 1945.)

retreats in a great wave and will probably run into our hands. In the evening we finally get something to eat. I go and get mine, taking it out of the pot. Our Lieutenant is standing there, and says: 'Prüller, don't fish out the best morsels as if you were at home.'

'At home I don't have to, sir. I get the best automatically.'

'Does she love you that much?'

'Certainly, Herr Oberleutnant.'

Don't you, Henny? You really do love me very much?

We spend the night dug into the field. We've had luck till now: it hasn't really rained yet. I'm still alive today, and so are you and Lore. All of us!

12th September 1939

At 4.00 a.m. we get up. We're relieved and move on towards Lemberg. My back aches so much after the night's discomfort that I can barely stand up straight. I've now had a wash, though. First time in five days! In the morning we have to go round a village (Krakowiec) because it's still being shelled by our artillery.

1.00 p.m.: two Polish planes shoot at us. Our flak draws a bead on them and one is hit. Two German fighter planes suddenly appear, chase the remaining Pole, and a minute later he is shot down in flames. A short but wonderful drama!

At 16.00 we call a halt, and have done just 20 kilometres. We skirt round a village in which there's still fighting going on. I've just heard a new rumour: in Germany there's supposed to be general mobilization. England and her Dominions are supposed to have declared war on us.

I consider this nonsense. For there isn't much left of Poland. And who would England and France fulfil their obligation to? It's too late for that. This is the trouble with this war: you never hear anything and have to depend on rumours. One day there was a soldiers' newspaper, specially for us . . . but only once!

A Kamerad, who got lost with his car, was shot by the Poles.

The people in the car, who had no weapons, were able to escape. Markl and his car have been missing for a week. He went to Division and hasn't returned since then. Another car, which broke down on the road and was picked up a few days later, was only a skeleton. A civilian we arrested was let out after he wept profusely, and when he got out he went into the nearest woods and shot at us again. A motor-cycle driver, who was repairing his vehicle, was foully murdered on the road. His body was completely disfigured. Seven soldiers who were waiting for the signal to proceed in their car were attacked by the entire village population, their eyes gouged out and castrated. A Red Cross convoy, doctors and assistants, wounded—180 men strong—not one of them armed, were murdered. 'Murdered' isn't the word for it!

These are the only 'deeds' the Poles have to boast of.

Cowards, cowards, they are! You can hardly get them to fight a decent fight. But they are very good at murdering! If an armed civilian crosses my path, I'll cut off his head with my own hands. I swear I will!

We've already driven through a number of villages and everywhere it was the same picture: Houses which had been hit by our artillery and set on fire. Homeless families, weeping women and children, who face the future with nothing. I don't think that the responsible gentlemen of the Polish Government who in their madness have called down this distress and misery on the Polish people, can ever answer sufficiently for their actions.

I accuse Minister Smigly-Rydz of having committed a shameless fraud in a most irresponsible fashion. I should almost like to say this: we are not fighting for our own rights alone. We are really fighting for the poor Polish people, too, from whom the ruling clique has withheld any sort of civilization and culture. Imagine a town of 30,000 inhabitants without even granite or stone-laid streets, much less an asphalt street. Dust. Nothing but dust. You just have to look at the houses the Polish peasant population is forced to live in, you just have to consider the hundreds of thousands of illiterates here in Poland. It is quite natural that 'social progress' proceeds at exactly this pace. A man gets 70 Grsczy for a whole day's hard work on a farm. That's not even 40 Pfennig!

So it is now our job to free the Polish people from all this wretchedness and, under our leadership, to make it into one of the happiest nations on earth.

In the evening we go on. Till 3 o'clock in the morning. Even then we haven't covered much ground, really. Through the detours, the bad roads with no light, an accident threatening every ten minutes. The ammunition truck of the heavy MG column crashed down a four-yard slope. Today I'm still alive, and so are you and Lore. All of us!

13th September 1939

We don't get very far. We draw up in the next village. A few hours ago, a Polish engineering unit pulled up stakes, leaving behind pontoons, their heavy MGs, their fighting equipment, even a radio. In no time we put the radio in working order. We hear news from Lemberg, supposedly the only Polish station still in action. It tells us that German troops have been cleared from the suburbs of Warsaw, that English planes are bombing Berlin every day, that French flak near the border shot down a lot of German bombers, that German troops are 260 km. from Lemberg and encircled by Polish troops. . . .

All lies and slander. We, for instance, are exactly 65 km. from Lemberg, as the road sign right in front of us informs us. Afterwards we listen to dance music. That does you good during a war!

In the morning we take up our position, because we're not sure whether the Poles will return. We buy milk and eggs. At 14.00 hours we move on, towards Lemberg. . . . At 16.00 hours we call a halt. Markl catches up with us. Thank God! Our Lieutenant comes to bring us the news that Lemberg has just fallen. We shall certainly go somewhere else now.

During the night we had an amusing experience: at 21.00 hours our Squadron had to dismount. At Rawa Ruska our Division took up its position. In the surrounding countryside there are supposed to be some Poles, who won't surrender. Supposedly cavalry. Some natives show us the way. We get as far as a forest, there's still nothing. So we hold a conference. Actually, it's dangerous to comb the woods in pitch darkness. Half an hour the discussion goes on, with pros and cons. We comb the woods. Nothing. At the top of the rise the troops meet and together we move on to the next forest. There a hand grenade is thrown into the woods. A lot of yelling ahead of us. A bunch of Poles stand up and ask us, gesticulating wildly, not to harm them. They surrender. There are 8 Polish soldiers, who have long since ditched their weapons. They were peacefully sleeping in the straw, didn't hear us at all, and were first wakened by the noise of the hand grenade exploding.

Our whole Squadron, about 250 men, can pride itself on capturing eight unarmed men! Of course, we were very annoyed.

At 23.30 hours we return to the vehicles and sleep as well as we can. Today I'm still living, and so are you and Lore! All three of us!

15th September 1939

As we were entering the town [Hrubieszow] yesterday, I noticed that the population lined the streets and raised their hands to show they had surrendered. Today I learn that they were expecting Polish troops. You can just imagine how wry their expressions were!

At 11.30 we move on, towards Chelm. In a village we are shot at. We storm the village. The enemy has withdrawn across a river to the other side of the village. My men and I follow him, while the others comb the houses of the village. For two full hours I lie there with my men and fight the enemy.

The Oberleutnant comes to me after some hours; at 18.00 I am relieved. In the afternoon all the Jewish shops are forced open, and the civilian population plunders them. You couldn't get chocolate or cigarettes anywhere.

In the evening we moved on. Before we took up our position, a murderous cross-fire began: the Poles tried a *tour de force* with much yelling and wanted to storm the village. Naturally they were beaten back. We had to spend the night in the open field. Today I'm still alive, and so are you and Lore! All of us!

16th September 1939

At 3.00 a.m. our artillery began to fire. I doubt if a single stone of the next village remained intact. Polish bombers have just tried to get us, but our flak was promptly at them and the Poles disappeared at once.

In the morning we went back a little and took another road, the best one that we've ridden on since 1st September. Well paved and, most important, dust-free. Our clothes and bodies are usually covered with a solid cake of dust after a few minutes' driving.

That was really something, tonight. The bullets just whistled! It's a curious feeling to hear the bullets above and next to you without ever knowing if they'll get you. When you hear them, you drop flat on the ground—at least during the first shots. Or take mortar or artillery fire: you hear them coming a long way off. And never a clue where they'll land. There really isn't any proper cover when you're in the open. Well, however fate wills it, that's the way it'll be. There's nothing to do but cross your fingers. If God pleases, I'll come home wounded, or healthy and untouched, or . . . not at all. We shall see.

14.30: we have arrived in a largish town, Zamosc. The entrance to it is surrounded by lines of trenches which the Poles threw up. The first houses are completely destroyed by our artillery: a horrid sight.

It's midnight already. Today I'm still alive, and so are you and Lore. All of us!

17th September 1939

At 1.00 a.m. we finally got a hot evening meal: black coffee! At 4.00 we're up again and pushing our positions forward. I'm so sleepy that I don't think I can stand it. Altogether it wouldn't be true if I said we slept more than 15 hours during this last week. It's already very hard to stand upright during the day, the last three weeks have been so incredibly exhausting. If we sit in our vehicles, our arses begin to hurt so much after half an hour that we have to stand again. It would be so good to be able to walk a few miles.

I almost forgot to say that 2 Polish soldiers of German Volksdeutsche ancestry are fighting with us; they came to us voluntarily and are the best of Kameraden.

Today is Sunday. Do you remember, Henny, how often I wanted to hear the Hafenkonzert[1] on Sundays and was too tired to stay awake? Now I've been lying in mud for three Sundays and would be only too happy to be home, lying in bed and listening to the radio. You have to go through a lot during a war, but you get hard and immune to everything. And those who haven't fought on the front don't know what war is. True, there are other things that have to be done, and there have to be people to do them. But the front is the front. That's without question, and there's no going soft here. I see it with us all the time.

Two of our officers have requisitioned a private car and are tearing around the country in it. Each of them has put on 15 kilos. And we? Trousers which we couldn't even squeeze into before are now too big for us. But despite it all, I don't want to leave the front—under no circumstances. If I were to be wounded and recover, I should be the first to go forward again; and I'd be delighted.

Today I'm still alive, and so are you and Lore. All of us!

18th September 1939

It rained hard during the night. It's tough to have to lie in the field and keep watch without any cover from the rain. And we were supposed to be relieved yesterday.

[1] A popular Sunday morning concert, consisting of marches, folk songs, etc., given by various bands of the German harbour cities (e.g. Lübeck, Hamburg, Bremen, and so forth) and broadcast over the whole *Reichsrundfunk*, including Radio Wien (Vienna), where Prüller would have heard it.

This is what we now get to eat—at the most impossible times. Black coffee for breakfast, though we usually don't get it at all. For lunch: a warm Eintopf,[1] which we generally get at dusk or during the night. For dinner: tea, and we get it at 1 or 2 a.m. You can imagine how full we are! This isn't a general mistake on the part of the Wehrmacht, however, for the error originates in the smallest unit—in our case it's our squadron.

We are told that soldiers of the Soviet Union have occupied Poland up to the River Bug. Their aeroplanes are marked with the Soviet star, their lorries are supposed to have an inverted swastika on them. This will mean the end of Poland. Warsaw is supposedly not yet taken, but completely encircled. The Führer is said to have given them twelve hours to evacuate Warsaw, after which time it will be attacked, with the help of the heaviest artillery and bombers.

This is the way the rumours go. Most of them are supposed to be authentic, often they're actually picked up by our radio transmitter car. We change our positions several times. This means a lot of work, because we have to dig ourselves in again each time. A deep hole, in which you can lie and, if the occasion warrants, spend the night. If you have any luck, there's some straw nearby, that you can pad out the hole with; it's not so cold then.

I'm already very cold. I shall go to sleep. Today I'm still alive, and so are you and Lore! All of us!

19th September 1939

At 6.00 a.m. every inch of my body was shaking with the cold. It drizzled the whole night and everything was cloaked in fog. The straw and our coats were soaking wet, and what's more, my blanket has disappeared. They've forgotten to feed my men since yesterday morning. We haven't been able to wash since Saturday. And to cap it all, my watch is broken.

We're supposed to have encircled 7 Polish divisions, who are

[1] A hot-pot, usually a sort of stew, containing a mixture of meat and vegetables.

hidden in the surrounding villages and woods, and are being bombarded by our heavy artillery. They should surrender, for there's no point in their going on with it.

Our flyers have dropped leaflets over the Poles, in which they are told that Russian soldiers have pushed 70 km. into Poland, that the Bug River is to be the demarcation line between the Soviet Union and Germany, and that the Poles should give up their resistance, lay down their arms and come over to us; nothing will happen to any of them, nothing whatsoever.

A large majority of the Poles don't dare to surrender because their officers tell them that they'll be shot by us, tortured, &c., which is of course pure rubbish. Quite the contrary; they are specially well treated. Nothing happens to any of them, not even a harsh word, whereas the Poles do the vilest things with our people. I'm surprised that the Polish officers—they are supposed to be men of character—allow such things to happen. But if you know that the Polish officers simply leave their men sitting high and dry in the most dangerous situations, then you understand it all. The day before yesterday, when we captured more than 100 prisoners, they themselves told us what had happened: when our tanks drove into the forest, the officers disappeared and left their men alone, and some of them came over to us.

Our artillery has been roaring away since 3 in the morning. The Poles are completely encircled, and there's no way out for them. But what good does that do us? These troops will surrender, and afterwards we'll get another order at once. For us, as a rush division, there will be no peace till the war is completely finished. And how long will that be? My dear Henny, I hope it will not be all too long. Fourteen days? A month? Or longer?

It's in the nature of things that it will be increasingly difficult for us as the autumn progresses, and as it gets steadily colder and wetter. Up to now the nights have been icy cold and the days boiling hot, but now there is no more sun during the day. Even now we have to keep our coats on all the time. I'm only surprised that up to now none of us has become seriously ill.

How often I've thought of home! On Sunday at 5.00 in the

afternoon I had such an attack of hiccups that I was positive you must have been thinking of me. And in my thoughts I imagined you sitting at home over coffee and thinking of your Manki.[1] And can you imagine how often I think of home leave? The surprise! The wild joy! The celebrations! Then a bath and sleep. Sleep! Because I'm so tired. For my first meal I want chicken in paprika. And then to be telling you everything: that's going to take a bit of time, isn't it?

Every day we take more prisoners, who come out of the woods on their own initiative. Some of the soldiers were left in the lurch by their officers and are now wandering round in the woods. Some of them were forced at pistol point by the officers, who are mostly Jewish, to go on fighting! Towards evening I capture 26 prisoners; some of them speak German well. I talk to them while taking them to the prisoners' camp, and learn a number of interesting things, mostly a confirmation of that which we already knew from the Poles. In the prisoners' camp I listen to the Führer speaking—just a few sentences intended for the English. Later I hear from many sides that the Führer declared the cleaning up of the Polish war to be a question of only a few days.

Today I'm still alive, and so are you and Lore. All of us!

20th September 1939

I look forward very much to the day when I can type these 'notes for a diary',[2] and then keep them properly. The interesting thing about this diary is that it was written while we were in position, often under the heaviest enemy fire; for what I want, in case anything happens, is that you will be able through this diary, my dear Henny, to learn what I was doing up to the last minute. . . .

13.00: I am looking at the countryside through my binoculars. Have the Poles surrendered?

13.30: Not a shot has been fired for two hours. And then—can

[1] Henny's pet name for Prüller.

[2] Herr Prüller in fact found time to do so.

you believe it! Polish soldiers are coming out of the woods, endless rows of 'em! Polish heavy guns are being carted off by our soldiers. Lorries are already moving to the woods to take the prisoners away.

21st September 1939

I have been captured by the Poles! I don't know what will happen. I and my men and our guards are lying between German and Polish fire. A Pole has just been badly wounded.

Our troop was woken up early in the morning. Yesterday evening a Polish rider appeared and said that in some woods about ten kilometres away were some 400 or 500 soldiers who wanted to surrender. We had meanwhile withdrawn to a town called Lasczow. Our Oberleutnant gave Stuparits[1] the order to send my troop to get the soldiers. A single-seater motor-cycle and one with a sidecar were assigned to us. At 5.00 a.m. we left.

The Polish rider went with us in the sidecar. At the place he described we dropped him off and waited for the Polish soldiers. A quarter of an hour or more went by. Our M/C combination went ahead to see what was happening. The fog was so thick that you couldn't see thirty metres ahead of you.

Suddenly the sidecar driver and the interpreter who was riding with him saw armed Poles advancing towards us. When he told us this, we mounted and withdrew a bit. A few minutes later some Poles actually showed up and gave themselves up. We took them along on our vehicle,[2] and on the way back we kept losing time by having to pick up more Poles.

When we got to the crossroads, about four kilometres from our troop, we heard an MG firing right next to us. We had to stop. When we wanted to go on, the motor wouldn't start. It must have been hit. The MG was firing like mad. We went behind a hill and waited. The town lay to the left in front of us, to the right were huge swamps.

[1] Stuparits had meanwhile returned to his unit, his wounds apparently healed.

[2] There must have been a lorry, apart from the motor-cycle and motor-cycle with sidecar.

Then, from the side where we intended to take the prisoners, appeared Polish soldiers, all armed. Before we could take this in, Poles appeared from the town side as well. Did they want to surrender? Anyway I bring my MG into position, but find I can use it only in one direction. No point in shooting because the Poles are swarming in from all sides. In short we are surrounded . . . and disarmed.

We are made to follow them towards the right, into the swamp. The Poles are about company strength. Five soldiers are assigned to watch us. Then our MGs begin to shoot at the Poles from the direction of the town: the noise is stupendous, the bullets whistle past us and over our heads. We're sinking up to our chests in the swamp, and it takes a long time for us to advance several hundred metres. And all the while we're being shot at by our own side.

We come through some tall reeds. On the other side is a little wall, and there we take cover. The Poles cross over the wall and receive tremendous fire from that side, while our people are shooting at us from the other. Then the German mortars go into action. The shells land all round us, some of them 10 metres away. It's a terrible feeling to think you might get shot to pieces by your own troops.

The leader of the guards, a young chap, climbs on the wall. On the other side, soldiers are approaching. Enormous numbers. We can't see if they're German or Polish. In any case they shoot at us. The Pole who first climbed on the wall is hit by a whole round of MG fire, one shot through the penis, two in his legs. He's bleeding like a stuck pig and is in terrible agony. We bandage him. The other Poles hope that the advancing soldiers are ours. They want to be taken prisoner. But it's Polish cavalry that now appears.

As they approach, they are raked by fire from our emplacements in the town, mortars, artillery, MG. We are lying helpless between two attacks. It goes on for hours. Finally the Polish cavalry troops approach us. We drag the wounded man back. He is in frightful pain and thinks it's all up with him. He tells us that his fiancée is Viennese. We promise to tell her what happened as soon as we get back. Though I think he'll recover. We carry him back across the swamps, again up to our chests in water. Then we go and get the other wounded: shot through the chest, the belly, the head . . . I shall spare you a description. Anyone who hasn't seen it can never imagine how terrible it is to get hit that way.

Then we are led to the Polish commander. Curiously, not all of us are searched. Whatever they found, they took.[1] Money, too. The officer makes us form a line. Exactly as many Polish soldiers, armed with carbines, march up to face us. We are made to turn. I think it's all up with me, then . . . I bid farewell to you and Lore . . . my spirit is dead already . . . two minutes this went on; it seemed to last twenty years. Then . . . about face. It is explained to us that we are prisoners of war. If we escape, we shall be shot. Obviously.

Then we're put on a lorry and taken to another command. There are now fifteen of us. We get some coffee with milk, and then we go to sleep in the hay. This was the worst day of all; I can tell you more when I see you. I'm actually dead, and it's only by chance that I'm still alive; and thus so are you and Lore! All of us!

22nd September 1939

In the morning we are led away again. I must say that many Polish officers with whom we are in contact behave most correctly. It is promised that not a hair of our heads shall be harmed, and if anyone mistreats us, we should protest to a Polish officer.

Many of them are actually human beings!

We get a little something to eat now. The trouble is, no one knows what to do with us. We wander from south to north, from east to west. On the roads we are continually harassed by Polish troops. But no matter whom we speak to, they all hope the war

[1] Prüller hid this diary next to his skin, and though he was searched, the diary was not found. While a prisoner, he wrote the entries whenever the Polish guards were not looking or, using a candle stump, at night.

will end soon. Nothing more to eat in the evening. Today I'm still alive, and so are you and Lore. All of us!

23rd September 1939

We have to go on, without food. Supposedly 6 km. We march towards the north. Have to turn back. Then eastwards, then westwards. We have more and more the feeling that the Poles don't know what to do with us.

The Poles' behaviour is good, now and then. What do you think is the explanation? We get nothing to eat all day long. Towards evening we arrive at a large farmhouse, where there are Polish troops as well. A captain receives us; he is exceedingly friendly. But food? Well, they haven't got any themselves. No flour. No salt. No bread. No fat. They've nothing. For some time they've been cut off from the others. He has a soup cooked up for us, made of corn and potatoes. It tastes ghastly. But it's warm. Then he clears out a room for us twenty-two prisoners. (I forgot to tell you that some days ago we were increased by seven more.) We go and get straw for the room. At last, a roof over our heads.

In the evening this Polish captain comes and sits with us. He speaks openly. A Polish officer with twenty-two captured German soldiers! He tells us his life history. He was born in Graz, has a wife and child. In the World War he fought for Austria and was wounded. He now lives in Lemberg, and his name is Alfred Teuer. Conversation turns to the present war. Which is lost for Poland, as he says. He speaks of an army which ran away. Of a force ruined and divided. Of England's guilt. Of fleeing officers. He knows the situation exactly. He's aware of everything. He says that though the war is as good as finished for Poland, for Germany it will go on. And he's right.

The war will continue until England's supremacy is crushed. He then promises to send us back to our front with an escort. He even wanted to let us go free this evening, but we thanked him and refused, thinking it might be dangerous. But he could not give us a statement that we asked for, saying that we were free and could return to our troops. We believed him, though, because a major had already said the same thing. We are already delighted at the prospect of being with our own people again. Today I'm still alive, and so are you and Lore. All of us!

24th September 1939

When we woke up in the morning, we found ourselves alone. The captain and his men have gone. So it's no 'back to the front, MARCH' for us! Other Polish troops soon arrive, however. All those we speak to, and whose outlook is not too limited, know that the war is lost for them. Despite the rumours, which are the same everywhere: only the method is different. All of them are sick and tired of fighting, and all wait only the end of Poland. The Germans, too. We are told that three Polish divisions were crushed today.

Civilians come to us. We buy bread, order a potato soup to be made and buy a goose which will be cooked for us; after all, today is Sunday.

Oh yes, I forgot to relate how one of our noncoms, when he was taken prisoner, was relieved of 180 Zloty. Captain Teuer gave them back to him yesterday: out of his own pocket, I'm sure. We were astounded. For the last day we've not had anything to smoke. We buy tobacco leaves and cut them up.

A Polish soldier saw six German tanks on a rise. If only our people would come! Our front is seven kilometres from here. We talk with the Polish soldiers; many of them can speak German, mostly Jews. In the evening, the Polish lieutenant lets us know that we shall have to accompany his troops.

At 5.30 we line up, and at 7.00 we leave. After one hundred metres we halt, to stay there for an hour and a half. Despite the wintry cold. Then we are sent back to our room. But we have hardly lit a fire, when we have to leave again. This time it's a false alarm, too. We come back; then actually leave for good half an hour later.

I ask the lieutenant what he intends to do with us. He explains to me sarcastically that we'll arrive in good time at the proper place. And that the schedule will be adhered to precisely. Just what does that mean? I advise everyone to be alert. To be a prisoner, a real prisoner, really is very hard, especially under such circumstances. They ought to send us to a general collecting point; after all, we can't be the *only* German prisoners. Or? And we haven't had anything decent to eat for God knows how long. And of course there's no hope of cigarettes.

Today I'm still alive, and so are you and Lore. All three of us!

25th September 1939

Today is another day full of nerve-racking events, if I count the night as well. One is much like the other. We had to march with the Poles the whole night, despite pouring rain.

Wherever we look, German beacons, searchlights. Germans. We march and march. There's practically no way out for the Poles. I have already decided that if the Polish lieutenant doesn't let us free tomorrow, I shall demand my rights of war. We must be brought to a camp, behind the lines. If there isn't any more 'behind the lines', then we must have a guarantee for our personal safety, which is a right we have as prisoners, and which we then won't have any more. We must be protected from the revenge of Polish soldiers.

As light comes, we see that the Poles have been able to break through the circle; for otherwise we would have already run into the Germans. I hope our tanks will arrive. But it seems too late for that. We turn into a forest, and there we'll probably remain till evening. With no food. The one hundred and forty Poles haven't any either.

It's still raining. I crawl behind a tree, while the Poles bring their horses and wagons and guns into the woods. Then I notice that a civilian with his arms raised comes out of the woods. Now another Pole! Then another!—I don't know how many! Why, all of them!

We twenty-two prisoners make a break for it. It's our only hope. Are the Germans coming? Or Ukrainians? It's a foreign command anyhow! As I get out of the woods, I recognize them: *They are our Russian allies!*

I can't describe this moment. The emotions inside me can't be described. I felt no joy. I didn't laugh. Or cry. Or weep. I wasn't touched at all. Only someone who rises from the dead can know this feeling.

It was three Russians who took the Poles prisoners, one officer and two noncoms. They saw the Poles coming, hid in the bush, and when the Poles were in the woods, the Russians began to shoot. No one had thought of opposition. Whereupon the Polish officers took to their heels, and the men, one and all, came out of the woods. The Russian captain at once gave us arms. We're full-value soldiers again! The numerous wagons are emptied and the contents sorted. This keeps us busy till 14.00. Then we help the captain cart the things off. We're off for Tomaszow, a town already in our hands.

In the evening we get an excellent soup, with lots of game and poultry in it. After the meal we push on. I haven't slept at all since yesterday morning. But perhaps I shall today?

26th September 1939

We drove right through the night. When the Russians take a breather, they do it differently from our way. They go up on a rise, where they can get a view of the whole surrounding country. *We* are always in a village or in a wood, to be out of sight of the planes. Or: when the Russians go through a village or a forest, they first shoot off a few MG shots, as a precaution against being killed by single pot-shots, but we don't do that. We've had to drive the Polish wagons. You can imagine what it's like to drive horses, when you've (as I haven't) no idea at all how to. To feed the horses, get them harnessed and unharnessed, it was awful.

The way the Russians treat us is not quite the way we would like. But the main point is, we're saved. The food is excellent, but unusual for us. They're simply altogether different people from ourselves. And very frugal.

We're supposed to go on this evening. And we actually do. It began to rain in the morning, and it's still raining.

27th September 1939

In pouring rain we travelled through the whole night. This morning we're supposed to reach Zamosc. There the Russian captain will pick up new orders. What we'd like best is if they would leave us in some town or other, and then send us back home. But not what is going on now! It's still raining. We are driving towards Lublin. Later we turn off and stop in a village. There the captain delivers us to staff. Up to now he's led us round any way he wanted to, and when we asked a question, he always found a new way of fobbing us off. The new captain—his name is Kavalenko—is quite different. He explains that we aren't prisoners but guests of the Russian Army. And that we'll go with the Russians until they meet up with German troops. The truth at last! It can't last more than two or three days, or a week. He's very friendly. They brought us food right away, and he gave us his own tobacco. Later they brought us dinner.

We stay in the village. At long last, a good night's sleep. We're simply exhausted.

28th September 1939

At 6.30 we get up. The rain, thank God, has stopped. In the morning we each receive a package of tobacco. It's a horrible weed, but it's something to smoke. Our clothes and underclothes, in so far as we have such things still, are completely soaked through. If I can only avoid falling ill! Not that!

The Russians push on again. The Germans are leaving this area. I just don't understand that. What was the battle of Tomaszow for? It cost us numberless casualties; and now it's to be Russian territory. I'm curious to see the Russian-German lines.

Yesterday we were told that the war was actually finished. Both armies are only cleaning up. We see this on the roads.

Thousands of Polish soldiers, their weapons surrendered, are going home.

That's typical of this war: people who are actually prisoners wander around free as birds. Do they just take their weapons away and send them back home? Or is it just the Russians who do that?

Actually I think it doesn't matter much to the Polish people whom they belong to. It was crazy of the Government to start the war. Now Poland has ceased to exist. Its beaten army moves in rows of thousands and thousands along the road.

All those I spoke to complained that the Polish officers ran away at the decisive moment. That's why they lost the war before they started. With a mentality like that!

During the night a guard was posted in front of our house, but they explained to us at once that it wasn't to guard us, but as an honorary measure to protect us from the civilian population. Quite something!

The Russian weapons are, in quantity, quite terrific. But do they measure up to the most modern technical standards? For the most part they are motorized. In general I think I can say: certainly no comparison with us. The best and most modern, the most disciplined and best trained army is that of Greater Germany [Grossdeutschland]. I'm only afraid of one thing, my darling Henny:

When our regiment returns to Vienna and I'm not with it, you'll be afraid I've been killed. I'm sorry about that. Your griefs, your worries. I don't even want to think of it. I hope the Russians will let you know, through the German authorities. Otherwise we'll be considered missing till we get back home.

The Russians are very charming hosts. They wait on us hand and foot.

29th September 1939

The food is gargantuan. In the morning some kind of soup and tea. At noon soup with meat and something to go with it. Evenings, meat soup and tea. The food is far superior to ours.

The soup all by itself is quite as good and as nourishing as a whole meal of ours. But we couldn't take it over a longer period. It's the same, too, every day. We get the sugar for our tea separately. The Russians put the sugar in their mouths and drink their tea that way.

The only hardship is the cigarettes. We each got a packet of tobacco, that's true. But there's no cigarette paper. We roll our cigarettes in a newspaper. The tobacco is so bad, though, that I don't smoke more than two or three cigarettes a day.

Yesterday we marched twenty-six kilometres and my legs ache all over. Today towards noon we marched off again and have to do another twenty-six kilometres.

30th September 1939

This morning I was terribly ill. I think that I'm no longer used to the filling and punctual meals.

We're supposed to have only twenty kilometres march to the Weichsel River. There we are to meet up with German soldiers and we will be with our unit today or tomorrow.

Ribbentrop is supposed to be with Stalin. They are reported to have signed some kind of arms agreement between the Soviet Union and Germany. I think that the Russians are keeping us back as a propaganda move, so that we'll say how well the Russians treated us. The troops in front of us are supposed to have already made contact with our army and told them about us.

Today we heard the latest news on the wireless. France is reported to have attacked German towns again, and French troops to have touched German soil. The troops, a thousand strong, were driven off. Otherwise all quiet. Russia is supposed to be working hand in glove with us now, and to have declared to France and England that if they attack Germany, they will find Russia on our side. The agreement is supposed to be binding for Germany, too. And so I think that the gentlemen in France and England will have to think things over carefully before they act so stupidly.

Moreover Papen is supposed to be in Paris. He will certainly produce some results.

1st October 1939

Smigly-Rydz has declared that the Polish Army is now defeated. He could have made this silly observation on 1st September! For it was a joke to fight against us with horse-drawn wagons. I've seen only very few trucks or tanks in the Polish Army, and aeroplanes only at the beginning. And with their weapons they can't compare with us at all. If their hand grenades were distributed to their whole army, it would mean two hand grenades for thirty-five men! Or take the company which took us prisoner: they had one MG! It was ridiculous!

They were terrified of our flyers. How right they were! When necessary they pulverized the Poles. When we were prisoners, we were often reproached for the fact that our flyers bombed the civilian population in towns, and refugees. That may have been true, but the reason is this: a reconnaissance plane takes photographs of the towns in which there are military objectives, railway yards, &c. The bombers then fly according to these photographs, and at the designated point the bombs are unloaded, without the pilot's having—in this case—to find out what's going on down below. If civilians happen to be underneath, it's not his fault.

When the Poles saw our flyers even at a great distance, they rushed off in all directions without paying any attention to us prisoners. But we twenty-two men didn't even think of escaping, for where could we go?

Yesterday I spoke to a Russian soldier who knew German. About conditions in Russia. Even if the picture we made, or rather which was made for us, was not correct, I nevertheless think that Communism for Russia was at that time her salvation; for the rest of Europe, and Germany in particular, it would be unthinkable. As time goes on, Communism will also forget its international ideas and become nationally conscious. Even now one speaks of our blood brothers in the Ukraine. Perhaps a Russian fascism will come to pass one day.

12.00: German officers came to the Russians for a staff conference. They are from the 27th Division. The Russians provide us with a truck and our officers take us along with them. Our own division is said to have withdrawn a considerable distance.

We're taken to Krasnik. But here we learn to our regret that no one knows where our division is, and we shall therefore be attached to the 63rd Infantry Regiment. We eat a good meal again, and in the evening we sit for hours with our Kameraden of the 63rd in front of an open fire and talk about our experiences.

2nd October 1939

Today we shall be posted. I'm curious to know where they'll put us and whether we shall all stay together. At noon there was, at long last, a real German meal again: beef soup, potato goulasch and black coffee. How good it tasted! After lunch we have to prepare ourselves, and are posted to the different units.

We look for new quarters and find them, too: rooms in a stone house, each one with a stove. There are even beds. In the evening we talk in bed for hours and describe our past lives. Again we come nearer to each other. I have to say it once again: there is something wonderful in this sense of comradeship within a group. We hold and will hold together, come what may. We go to sleep late, each of us wishing to be with our dear ones again soon.

3rd October 1939

We put our modest dwelling in order, heat the stoves, and then go to wash. When the Poles were taken prisoner by the Russians, I organized[1] pyjama trousers and a shirt, so that at least I have a change of clothes. Then I go into town and have my hair cut. Now I look like a human being again. Some decent clothes, and I can go on for a while!

Yesterday the soldiers of the light infantry got their mail.

[1] The word used by the American army was 'moonlight requisitioning'.

Almost every one of them got a pile of letters and parcels. Can you imagine, Henny, how heavy my heart was? It's not easy, something like that. I couldn't help it, I had to go away. But I am happy that at least I could send a message to you, for who knows whether you weren't told that I was missing. I would like to write to you several times each day, but there's not a piece of writing-paper to be had, far less an envelope. The only shop that's open is the barber's. There's nothing to be bought, no fruit, no chocolate, no cigarettes, no clothes, nothing.

4th October 1939

We are now supposed not to be going to march, because the 1st Battalion is coming here. Then it's to go to Lublin. The Division remains as an occupation force in Poland. That would be terrible for us. In the afternoon they bring us to the 1st Battalion; we go to the commander and ask to be allowed to return to our troop. But we don't have any equipment and no proper clothes. I have silk pyjama trousers and a 'charmeuse' shirt,[1] no socks, dilapidated shoes instead of boots, no cap, no field canteen, no mess equipment, &c. It's the same for each of us.

The commander promises to transfer us as soon as they reach Lublin. It's a Bavarian regiment, and of course we understand each other very well. I've got a first-class cold, and hope it's not 'flu. That's all I need.

At 9.00 I go to the chief of the company we're attached to. He explains that we're only here as guests, that we won't really go on duty at all, and ought to be with our own people in a few days. Let's hope so.

5th October 1939

We are supposed to be ready to march at 9.00. From the Company we go to the Battalion, are loaded in lorries and leave

[1] A shirt, prevalent in Germany during the war, made of artificial silk.

for Lublin. There, we spend the night, forty of us in a room in a factory. Tomorrow we're to be put on the train, and will probably go to Vienna. That would be something! At least for a day. My God! A bath again. A white bed. And you . . . you . . . you . . . you!

6th October 1939

At 6.00 we leave for Radom. There we heard the Führer's speech. The end was really great. The people of Europe, especially France and England, should come to their senses at last; otherwise it could happen that . . . after all, Poland was once a state, too.

8th October 1939

At 6.00 a.m. we crossed the former German border. In Oppeln we changed trains for Breslau. Red Cross nurses treated us royally with coffee and bread-and-butter sandwiches. When the people on the station platforms found out that we had been prisoners, they handed us apples, chocolate and cakes through the window. In Breslau we again got a real reception from the Red Cross nurses. We were given good soup and coffee and bread and butter. How much less fortunate our fathers were in 1918.[1] At 13.30 the D-Zug[2] takes us towards our beloved Vienna. To wife and child. To parents.

In all the towns of the Reich, the flags of our nation adorn the windows: the visible sign that the war with Poland has been brought to a victorious end. It is a victory of indescribable importance. It is a victory of heroism, a victory of right. It is a victory of sacred belief in our eternal Germany, a victory of National Socialism, and thus a personal victory of Hitler.

For it was Adolf Hitler who cancelled the shameful debt of

[1] In 1918, many soldiers returning from the front were attacked by the war-weary population.

[2] The German equivalent of our express train.

Versailles for all of us, cancelled it in a way which at the beginning no one believed possible.

He put the German people, in this war against Poland, to the strongest test they have undergone since the World War. And now 82,000,000 Germans have fallen in to report to the Führer: 'Adolf Hitler! Thy German people have withstood this test!'

My dearly beloved Henny!

This diary was conceived while thinking of you. It was intended to show you the way, the difficulties, in fact everything that happened to me in the war. These pages were to be sent to you, were I no longer there. I am sure that these daily, nay hourly thoughts of you—together with your talisman[1]—protected me from death. I don't know, I always persuaded myself that I was immune against the enemy's fire.

The hours in which I saw you in my mind's eye, distorted with pain—these were difficult hours. Now that's finished. We must remain happy. God wanted it to be so. Let us thank Him.

Note:

There were of course many things that I couldn't really write about the way I wanted to, particularly during the period of my captivity. I had to be prepared to be searched once more by the Poles, or when I was with the Russians, to be taken prisoner once more. And then, there are many things which don't belong in these notes, which are intended only for you.

8th October 1939. On the trip between Breslau and Vienna.

6th November 1939

Twenty-four beautiful, wonderful days of leave are now at an end. What have they brought to both of us? For you, some evenings when you were alone, that's the bad side of it. And some wonderful, I think very wonderful hours. For me, the same.

We heard a lot of news in this time: actually, only bad news—

[1] Herr Prüller informed us that the talisman was the umbilical cord of his child, Lore, wrapped in the leather case of his 'dog-tag'.

of the great number of my Kameraden who fell. It's awful. Just to think that Wallner, Kolschek, Hofer, Mohor, and Lord knows how many others, are no more. Kameraden, who shared their all with each of us, who threw their lives into the breach to save another. Well, such is fate. The man who knew how to worm out of everything, who escaped every kind of responsibility—he's generally in safety somewhere. The other gave for the nation the utmost that a person can give: his life. How awful it was when Hofer's parents were here at our place; and when I bought a quarter of a kilo of apples from Kolschek's parents and looked at his mother's eyes without letting her know who I was.

Yes, such is war. What more can be in store for us? We don't know.

2. THE WAR IN THE WEST, THE WAR IN THE BALKANS

Summary of and Extracts from the Diary, November 1939 to June 1941

[After his three weeks of leave, Prüller was sent to Lower Austria where he was posted to his old squadron; early in December his unit was sent to a training ground at Hammelburg, not far from Aschaffenburg in the Palatinate. There he heard, on 19th December, of the Luftwaffe's victory over forty-four English fighters and bombers near Wilhelmshaven the afternoon before, according to the official German version of which the British lost thirty-four of their planes. (Both sides exaggerated the enemy's losses in accounts of this sort; the exaggeration became particularly crass during the Battle of Britain.)]

As I was reading in bed at 22.40 hours, I heard the wireless going in the next room; the announcer was so excited that I thought there must be a special news broadcast. In my shirt and pants, I rushed into the next room and heard the report given by the commander of our fighter aircraft. . . . It's a wonderful show of arms! German energy paired with all the other virtues of our people have been responsible for this proud victory. And that's the way the final victory will be, too! For this reason: the others are fighting for a wrong cause, fighting to prevent us from living, fighting to keep us from enjoying the bounties of the world. We're fighting for our rights, for our lives.

And it is always those who are in the right who win.

And today we're a different Germany from what we were! A National Socialist Germany. And we know how to fight for our rights and lives. The gentlemen in London, and in Paris too, ought to put that in their pipes and smoke it! . . .

[In January 1940, Prüller's unit was again moved, this time to a village in the 'Saarpfalz' about 30 or 40 kilometres from the French border; in March, they were transferred near the German-Dutch border. On 21st March, Daladier resigned and Paul Reynaud was entrusted with forming a new government. In April, Germany occupied Norway and Denmark. Prüller writes:]

9th April 1940

In the afternoon the rumours [of the occupation] were confirmed. . . . It is the turning point of the war. . . . Our boys are really delighted. Dear God in Heaven, we thank Thee that we are Germans, and still more that we are allowed to live in this gigantic epoch. . . .

[On 18th April, Prüller was asked if he would like to transfer to Regimental Staff Headquarters. Prüller agreed, and writes:] On the one hand I am not too happy at having to leave my Kameraden, whom I've been together with for one and a half years; it's specially hard to have to leave our revered Herr Hauptmann [Captain]. But on the other hand, there are possibilities in the regiment which beckon to me—the kind of thing I always needed in my life. So I seized the opportunity. [Prüller had not had the best time of his military career in the last few months; he had been involved in a brawl, as a result of which he was arrested and 'thrown into the jug' for several days.

[On 9th May the regiment was placed on the alert. 'That's it!' writes Prüller; 'Hurrah!'. The next day the campaign in Belgium, France and Holland began. Prüller, now advanced to *Gefreiter* (lance-corporal in the British Army, private first class in the American), was attached as battle clerk to Regimental Staff Headquarters (C.O.: Oberstleutnant Reinisch) of Schützenregiment 11, part of the 9th Armoured Division (G.O.C.: Ritter von Hubicki) belonging to the *Armeegruppe* (group of Division) under General Ewald von Kleist.

[During the French Campaign, Prüller did not take an active part in the fighting: his *Schützenregiment* remained as a reserve unit, behind the lines. For this reason it was not thought necessary to include this section of the diary at all, since Prüller's knowledge of what was taking place was second- and third-hand. A few comments of political and sociological interest have been included:

Thursday, 16th May 1940

As far as I am informed about conditions in Holland—in Belgium it's much worse, I'm told, not to speak of France and England—it's quite clear to me that the Western powers are afraid of us. Perhaps not because of our National Socialist régime, and not only because we're Germans. No, they are afraid of our national orderliness, they are afraid of our sense of justice, of our proper economic efficiency, of our holidays, such as the 1st May, which they don't know about here. They are afraid of our German gift for organization, afraid of our German propaganda; afraid that their people will wake up by themselves and drive their rulers from the country with sticks, or drown them like dogs. That's what the gentlemen in London, Paris, Brussels, etc., are afraid of. But don't worry, gentlemen! Your hour is rapidly approaching, and any minute now you'll be in touching distance of us. Germany's coming all right; her Wehrmacht, at the head of which will be our dearly beloved Adolf Hitler! We'll find you, sure enough. . . .

Saturday, 18th May 1940

14.30 hours. A huge column of soldiers is approaching us from the opposite direction: Belgians and French, about 500 of them, on the road to Berlin. . . . Oh yes, Herr Daladier & Co., we'll present our little bill yet. The *Ostmärker* [i.e. Austrians] whom you were so sorry for! Perhaps you can convey your sympathies personally; my Kameraden and I would be just delighted to receive them. Or perhaps you're in London for good? Well, if you just wait a bit, we'll be there soon, too. . . .

. . . I simply can't explain how it's possible for two peoples only a few miles distant from each other to reveal such differences in culture, education, organization, and so on. In Holland: all things considered, a very pleasant surprise; in Belgium it's, simply *Polish*!

Sunday, 19th May 1940

In the most splendid spring sun, and in the thunder of battle in the west, you, dearest Henny, celebrate your first anniversary of motherhood. Surely on this day you will go to our little one's bed and look upon your own flesh and blood with transfigured eyes, and the child will beam at you happily. Its mother. Today without understanding, but later in the realization that it is a part of you, that it has grown up with the knowledge that it can turn to you with all its problems.

It's that way with everyone. Even when a man is old and grey, he is always lovingly attached to his mother. How many Kameraden, who gave up their lives in this gigantic, decisive battle [*Entscheidungsschlacht*] died with the word 'Mutter' on their lips. . . . Know, too, that you mothers have a national responsibility in war. . . . Be unswerving in the holy belief in this our rightful cause, be never wavering in your confidence in our dearly beloved Führer, be proud that your sons may take part in this, the greatest war in history. Be overjoyed if you may be permitted to sacrifice them for *Volk, Reich und Führer*. Be honest, true, German mothers!

Tuesday, 28th May 1940

11.30 hours. On our wireless we hear the news that the Belgian Army has surrendered unconditionally. My eyes are wet for joy and pride in the Wehrmacht's accomplishments, for respect and thankfulness at those who fell. Now comes the turn of those who are most to blame [French and English]. We'll get you. . . .

Monday, 10th June 1940

On the road we found a vehicle on its side—one from our artillery units. One soldier lay beside it, dead, with a knife in his chest, another was badly wounded but still alive. He told us they were attacked by mutinous negro prisoners and knifed. As a reprisal we rounded up 20 negroes and shot them on the spot. . . . In the evening we learn that Italy has declared war on France and England. . . .

Monday, 17th June 1940

In St. Saulge a woman addressed us in very good German—probably a Jewess!—and complimented us on our performance during the last three weeks. It really is incredible! We can scarcely believe it ourselves. . . . On Saturday, 18th May, I wrote some friendly advice for you, Herr Daladier, which can also serve for your successor, Reynaud. . . . I didn't know then that in scarcely five weeks Paris would be in our hands and your armies in complete disintegration. But one thing I *did* know: that the moment your armies gave in, you would run off, far away. That I did know. Herr Reynaud, you have the dubious distinction of having been at the head of your people in this its most historic moment; you have the dubious distinction of having plunged two peoples into utter chaos; you have the dubious distinction of having shamefully betrayed your people and then fleeing.

You cannot turn back the wheel of history, Herr Reynaud, but the time will come when history will pass judgment on you in the way you deserve. . . . While we are marching a special announcement from the Führer's headquarters reaches us: Marshal Petain is considering an armistice. He asks the Führer for our terms. My God! we can't believe it. . . . I am so utterly happy. . . .

Monday, 24th June 1940

At 23.50 hours I hear a special announcement [on the wireless] that at 1.35 [a.m. on 25th June] all arms are to be laid down. The war in the West is ended. One of the most glorious victories in German history has been won! We've done it!

Tuesday, 25th June 1940

The first day of peace in the West. We don't expect any further advance today. Vehicles, weapons, machines are to be put in order. . . . I've still only one wish: to get to England. . . . From the 6th Comp. a parcel for Corporal Vraz [who fell] was returned to me. It's firmly packed and tied up with several bits of string. Quite heavy. I gaze at the parcel for a long time before I write on it, in red pencil: 'Gefallen für Grossdeutschland'. Then I send it back to his wife. What can be inside? Perhaps a cake with lots of raisins, he used to like that. Perhaps some apples. Some pictures from his beautiful Styria. Perhaps some good cigarettes. Vraz smoked only on Sundays. Perhaps a letter in which she tells him she's pregnant. Vraz has been married only a short while. Poor Vraz. Poor Vraz? No, brother. You are rich, immensely rich. You have given the best, the finest, the noblest for your fatherland. You have 'Fallen for greater Germany'.

[There follows an account of the trip back home, through Luxembourg and the Mosel valley, to Stuttgart, Munich, Braunau, Amstetten in Lower Austria, where they arrived on 6th July.]

Friday, 19th July 1940

21.00 hours. The ringing 'Heil' still in my ears, I leave the C.O.'s room, in which I just heard the Führer's speech.

In my mind's eye I see before me the field-grey uniforms of the Reichstag delegates; I see the thousands and thousands in the crowd waiting in front of the Kroll Opera House [Berlin] to give to the Führer and his men proof of the burning love of the people. Even now I hear the words which aroused everyone, and I sit down at my table with my own thoughts.

It excited me just as much as the whole German nation. . . . When you consider the progress of the last ten war months—the destruction of Poland, the heroic battle of Narvik, the capitulation of Holland and Belgium, the smashing of France—it is quite unbelievable. Here brilliant military strategy has been wedded to statesmanship of exceptional power; our marvellous Wehrmacht, so integrated, was forcefully supported by home production; but above everything else, how obvious it is that the Almighty has blessed us in this struggle!

We are aware of our strength! We know that at the conclusion of this struggle will be the most glorious victory of history; we fear nothing, no one. For after all, the Führer has said how incomparably we are armed for this last phase of the struggle, how immense are our arms and munition, our supplies, petrol and fuel, our inexhaustible fund of raw materials. . . .

But despite all this: once more the Führer has appealed to reason. As a soldier, as a human being, as victor! Once more he has given England and the world the possibility of ending this senseless battle. What a man!

I know, though, what will happen. You, Mr. Churchill, will once again describe this as the Reich's weakness. You will ignore this last appeal or gloss it over with an idiotic gesture. Probably you won't even feel the effects of this last struggle; in the final analysis only the English nation will feel it, just as it's always the people and not the criminal leaders who feel the effect.

We soldiers, we burn—just as our Führer said—to fight against England, our arch enemy! This is quite clear from everything I've written up to now. We want to avenge all the insults which she [England] has heaped upon the German people, and especially our soldiers; we want revenge for the ridicule she has heaped on our Führer; to avenge the murder of our women and children; and finally we want to force from her our right to live!

Give us this right to live of your own free will, Mr. Churchill, and you save the lives of millions of people; you will spare the English nation useless mountains of corpses; you will save the land from a devastation far worse than in France. Herr Churchill! Here is the hand of freedom, offered by the Führer in his deep sense of responsibility—and with it freedom and work and reconstruction. Or destruction and misery and need and an empire destroyed.

In both cases, however: now and for all time, an established greater German Reich!

Choose, Mr. Churchill!

[Shortly afterwards, Prüller went on leave. His unit subsequently moved to Vienna, and Prüller could sleep at home. The next months were a period of relaxation; it was not till the end of October that he had to leave Vienna, and then only to a training 'refresher' at Bruck. Meanwhile Prüller was advanced to *Unteroffizier* (N.C.O.). In January 1941 he learned that Roumania was to be his unit's next goal. There follow extracts from Prüller's Diary of the campaign in the Balkans:]

[Letter to Henny in Diary:]

Saturday, 1st February 1941

Tomorrow at 7.30 a.m. we shall leave Vienna, from the Bahnhof Stadlau. For the fourth time since my army life began I must take leave of you, without knowing when and if I shall return. . . . This time it's different, because you're expecting our second child [Heinz Peter, born 30th April 1941].

My God! How proud of you I am. How happy to know that I call one of the best, bravest and dearest of woman my own. And how happy and pleased I am with our little one—our sunshine. . . .

I leave you, and Lorli, and everything I hold dear, but it is not difficult to go. My duty calls me, my Führer. I am happy and pleased—I cannot repeat this enough—to be able to be where the German man can best show his true colours. And I know that in this period our fate for the next centuries is being decided. I commend you to God!

[*8th February 1941*]

The Hungarian population very friendly. In Temesvar I could

have bought salami, 8 Mark the kilo. . . . When we arrived in Roumania, one could see the difference in the people right away —thoroughly dirty, smeary characters. . . .

Sunday, 9th February 1941

It is strictly forbidden to buy goods and so on, and we're watched carefully. . . . It's no particular disadvantage, because only food is really cheap, everything else very expensive. A *Wiener Schnitzel* costs 32 Lei, a scrambled egg with ham 28 Lei, a pair of *Würstl* with mustard 24 Lei, a bottle of wine 50 Lei and so on; a suit 6 to 8,000 Lei. . . . We've got a fabulous rate of exchange, 1 Mark to 80 Lei (normal rate only 50 Lei).

Wednesday, 12th February 1941

When you see Roumanian soldiers, you are at once reminded of the way Polish, Belgian and French soldiers look. Very, very pathetic. . . . The Roumanian soldier gets 60 Lei a month. . . .

Monday, 24th February 1941

On Saturday last I made a surprise trip to Bucharest. We left with the motor-cycle at 2.00 p.m. and were there at 5.00. It got dark soon—Bucharest is completely blacked out—but I could see one thing: the immediate contrast between poor and rich; wonderful skyscrapers next to old, historic buildings; noise and traffic such as I've never seen elsewhere; undisciplined pedestrians who pay no attention at all to the numerous policemen, all blowing their whistles madly, or to the red lights. . . . In the evening I ate in an excellent restaurant; I paid 70 Lei for a pork chop with potatoes. . . .

Tuesday, 26th February 1941

We are to move to Bulgaria in march formation. . . .

Sunday, 2nd March 1941

At 12.00 we crossed the military bridge over the Danube between Giurgiu and Ruse. In Ruse itself, which lies right on the Danube and is our first Bulgarian town, we were heartily welcomed. Bulgarian soldiers salute very smartly. You notice right away a considerable difference between the Roumanian and Bulgarian troops. Flowers and cigarettes are thrown to us, and the people continually cried: 'Heil Hitler', 'Auf Wiedersehen', 'Gute Reise' and so forth. German and Bulgarian flags decorate the houses. . . . Again we soldiers find ourselves proud and happy to be Germans. It's a wonderful feeling to be a German soldier and be cheered like that. May each one of us realize that we can rightly be proud of ourselves, proud that the whole world looks at us in admiration. Kameraden! That's something to live up to!

Monday, 3rd March 1941

10.00 hours. We just drove through Gabrovo. No one thought the population here would be as charming as it is. Cigarettes, books, fruit, friendly greetings of 'Sieg Heil', 'Gute Reise' &c. in abundance. Beyond Gabrovo there's a factory built entirely according to our principles of 'beauty in work'. Bright, high windows, living quarters for the workers, a fine park, &c. Our influence is unmistakable.

Up to now I can only say that Roumania can't be compared in any way to Bulgaria. . . .

13th March 1941

There are some, though not many, soldiers here who have contracted venereal disease. That's of course disgusting, not only for the married men, but also for the single. How *can* one, as a German soldier, get involved with any old piece of tail in skirts whom one comes across? It's quite clear that the women involved are hardly decent. Obvious that those who contracted the disease don't realize they're Germans, and don't think what consequence such a thing can have for our people, and of course for themselves. Revolting!

15th March 1941

We've the offensive before us now. We're to go to Greece. . . .

Tuesday, 1st April 1941

The condition of the *Volksdeutsche* in Jugoslavia is becoming impossible to bear. Today two special trains with German refugees are supposed to have arrived in Graz. Reports of people being dragged away as in Poland, and so on. But a couple of days' patience, my dear Serbs, and we'll be coming. . . .

4th April 1941

This afternoon . . . we received orders to attack Jugoslavia. We shall not lay down our arms until the Jugoslav Government in its present state is crushed; until that destructive herd [*Unruheherd*], who set off the greatest blood bath of all times—the first World War—is 'taken care of' [Prüller's quotes]. . . .

Easter Sunday, 13th April 1941

We just learn that Belgrade has fallen. That's the end of the Jugoslav Government. . . .

Monday, 14th April 1941

At 03.00 hours we cross the Jugoslav-Grecian border. . . . To my astonishment I don't see the [Greek] soldiers surrendering, wandering round in our occupied zone without their guns, as we did in Poland, Holland, Belgium, France and Jugoslavia. Are they perhaps better soldiers than all the others?

18th April 1941

We found several severely wounded men. They had lain four days in the rain. The English didn't bandage a single one of them; on the contrary, they put them in the path of our artillery fire. The dying Kameraden were given water mixed with petrol. This scandalous act of the English at Stena Portas will never be forgotten![1]

[The details of Prüller's part in the action have been omitted here, since they are more or less a repetition of what he experienced in Poland. His comments on Greece, as he left the country, were:]

8th May 1941

At 03.00 hours we [re]cross the Grecian-Jugoslav border. I take my leave of a country which made absolutely no impression on me whatever. I was very disappointed. We could see nothing of Europe's old *Kulturland.* Greasy people and poor, impossible clay huts and houses. . . . We weren't in the real Greece, the historical part, but that won't be much better.

As far as I can judge, this nation is at least two thousand years behind and lives only from its age-old (if epoch-making) cultural tradition.

Again another country has fallen because of you, Herr Churchill, a country which you selected as a springboard against the unconquerable Reich. And as with the others, you shamefully betrayed it. We are only happy that the Greeks didn't have to make such a bloody sacrifice as did the French &c. . . . But even

[1] In fact the 'scandal of Stena Portas' naturally never happened. One of the N.C.O.s was wounded on the pass, and when discovered, told this story which he invented. He was cited in the dispatches and promoted. Later, when German prisoners (whom the British had captured at Stena Portas) were set free, they all said unanimously that they had been 'royally treated'. The 'scandal of Stena Portas' was then investigated, and the guilty N.C.O. brought before military court for trial. Prüller knew all this and said to the editors [S.L.] that he had 'corrected this in letters to his wife'; the passage in the diary remained, significantly, uncorrected.

these few were driven to death by you, Herr Churchill. When one day the history of the world's greatest war criminals will be written, you shall certainly have the questionable honour of first place among them.

[After moving back across Roumania and Hungary, where Prüller reports the German Army having been 'enthusiastically received everywhere', especially in Budapest, the Schützen-regiment moved into Austria, where the population greeted them with flowers and tears of joy. As the tanks rolled round the Gürtel in Vienna, one old woman gave them fistfuls of 1-Pfennig coins; 'Go buy yourselves a beer,' she said in her incredible Viennese dialect; 'You soldiers are always thirsty.' Prüller managed to squeeze in a short leave before his unit left for their next post in Friedland (Upper Silesia) on 17th May 1941, preparatory to the (highly secret) invasion of Soviet Russia. He also had a longer leave between then and 21st June, when the next section of the Diary, which we have printed with a few minor excisions, begins.]

3. THE WAR AGAINST THE SOVIET UNION

[Friedland, Upper Silesia] 21st June 1941

Tonight we're off, despite the fact that we haven't all our vehicles. We got a batch of new ones, and the ones that are still missing are supposed to be delivered today; I wonder; but it will work out, it always does.

I'm not sure yet what's happening. But we are to go to the East, and quite certainly to Russia later on. But as what? I cannot believe that the Führer would sign a non-aggression pact, only to break it two years later. On the other hand, though, we are supposed to prepare for air attacks, and they keep talking of troop concentrations. And if Molotov really gets pushed out and Stalin makes a deal with England, then of course it's clear that we've got to crack down. Personally what I think will happen is that they'll let us march through voluntarily. Anyway, we shall know in the next day or two.

I rang you up tonight, but you weren't in.

22nd June 1941

I had to work till 5 minutes before 4.00 a.m. and just had time to reach the C.O.'s car before we started. Some of the townspeople walked beside us and stood on the street till we were out of town. Many Kameraden received flowers and some sort of loving message, and with great waving of hands we left Friedland at 4.15.

It's a marvellous day, and you can see how healthy it is to drive away in the early morning. As I was trying to make out what was what, we heard at 6.00 that Germany, Roumania and Finland are, as of today, at war with Russia.

Some of us simply gaped with astonishment, some took it with equanimity, some are horrified; these latter are full of dire prophecies that it can't end well. Personally I think it's a good thing that we face the fight squarely and save our children from having to do it. For this reason: in the long run it would have proved impossible for two such giant nations, living right next to each other and with such completely different ways of life, to exist side by side in peace and understanding.

The fight between Communism, which is rotting so many peoples, and National Socialism was bound to come. And if we can win now, it's better than doing it later. And the Führer will know what he's doing. Above all, I'm sure it'll end well.

Right at the beginning of our march a sparrow befouled the radiator, and the Major ordered us to leave the droppings where they were: but if the vehicle has to be washed, then we're to wash round the crap. How we laughed at him! He bellows a lot and loudly, our chief, but he doesn't really mean it. And the aide-de-camp, too, is well known for being a sharp character, and only the driver, a wet-behind-the-ears noncom from Styria—very afraid and shy—he thinks the Major isn't a human being. But I'll teach him differently yet!

In Tschenstochov and in other larger towns too, the Jews are herded together in a particular part of the town—like our former Judengasse in Vienna. When they go out they (man or woman) have to wear a white armband with a blue star of Zion on it. That's the way it should be in the whole world!

As far as we can see from our lorries, the people in general are in a very depressed state. At least that's the outward impression you get. They all walk with their heads down. Huge queues wait for bread and milk. The Poles won't have a very rosy time of it!

At 13.45 we arrive in Demba, about 12 km. from Kosnic, and camp in the woods. It was very hot the whole day, and we're thirsty already. There's no drinking-water here, only a slimy pond that you wouldn't even want to wash yourself in. We didn't get any maps for today's march, nor for tomorrow's either, so we have to prepare map sketches for the companies. Late in the evening I got a complete set of maps for Russia, 10 huge parcels. What a job! Oh, well, I didn't get any sleep last night, I might as well stay up tonight, too.

In the afternoon we get marching orders for tomorrow. We're to get up early and push on to the division rendezvous at Krasnik. From now on we're to travel completely blacked out. Krasnik isn't far from the border.

Wednesday, 25th June 1941

They are making large-scale preparations for gas attacks. It's thought—also in the higher echelons—that the Russians will use gas. I hope the Führer is not so humane once again as not to order immediate retaliation. I can well imagine that when the Bolshevist way of life is about to be crushed, they will use any means to save themselves.

We're still waiting for marching orders. We are not at all pleased by these quiet days, first because we haven't any zloty and secondly because there's nothing to buy anyway, no bread, no wine, no cigarettes. The only cigarettes we could get were by trading eggs for them.

Friday, 27th June 1941

At last the time has come. Today at 18.00 we're to be ready to march, the orders say we're to leave at 21.00 for the region near Zamosc. Now those lousy night marches begin again!

Two days ago we learned that Minsk had been taken, and now Dubno has fallen, too. In the very first days more than 1,000 Soviet planes were shot down, that's about a quarter of all their workable machines. Isn't it natural that we can barely wait to go into action? After all, we want to have accomplished something big in this, our greatest and most important fight.

Our departure was delayed because all the roads ahead of us are stopped up, but at 23.30 we leave, moving very slowly forward. In the towns and villages the traces of the 1939 battles can still be seen. As we went through Bilgorey, the only thing you could say was, that *used to be* Bilgorey.

Sunday, 29th June 1941

At 9.30 we get our orders to march at 16.00. We shall probably cross the German-Russian border before Rava Ruska.

At 17.45 we go through Zamosc. Nearly two years ago I went through here with the Russians. How curious fate is. We are on the road to Rava Ruska now, and it's a first-rate one. I remember [in 1939] noticing that it was the only really good road I saw before I was taken prisoner by the Poles. Zolkiev is our next goal.

In the afternoon came the news of our tremendous successes: 40,000 prisoners, 4,107 enemy planes destroyed, 600 pieces of heavy artillery captured. But the coming days will bring even higher figures, for two Russian armies are encircled.

At 21.30 we cross the German-Russian border the other side of Belce. It's dark, but we could see the primitive Russian border defences. The farther we advance, however, the better the defences look. There, for instance, is a deep tank ditch, and when you get across it to the other side, there is a plateau just as long; then it drops straight down to the Russians, many metres. This trap is left and right of the road, on the right several hundred metres long, ending in a bunker which dominates the whole area; to the left it extends only some 50 metres—the Russians didn't get any farther than that.

The first two villages look very badly burned out: the usual picture. A number of Russian prisoners pass us: they certainly didn't imagine that the war would end this way for them. They don't even look at us.

We proceed a metre at a time. It's rotten driving like this, especially through Rava Ruska. At 2.30 in the morning while we're in Rava Ruska we get word on the radio that the advance road is impassable and we should halt and rest. It's not until 3.00 a.m. that I can lie down in my vehicle.

Monday, 30th June 1941

At 5.45 we're up again. Our major is to report to Regiment Headquarters. The road is the worst imaginable: deep sand and then huge craters right across the whole road, and this mile after mile. I write the orders on the road.

My eyes ache from looking at so many vehicles, one after the other as far as you can see. We arrive about 15.00, after travelling along these impossible roads, in Busk, where there's still fighting going on. The western entrance of the town is jammed full of our vehicles, and all you can see there is dust, but the Russian guns are still barking away at the eastern end. On the other side of the bridge an armoured scout car is burning; the bang of its ammunition covers the noise of our motored columns.

They are hauling some Russians out of the houses—disgusting creatures. Our colonel sits at a table, completely calm, and gives his orders. Among a batch of Russians who are in the process of surrendering we catch sight of a wounded, uniformed Russian woman. She's the first skirt in uniform we've seen in Russia so far. Neither Red Cross nurses, nor anything else, but actually soldiers!

This region has quite a lot of Ukrainians. In every village we're showered with bouquets of flowers, even more beautiful ones than we got when we entered Vienna. Really! It's true! In front of some villages they have erected triumphal arches. Some have the following inscription in Russian and German:

'The Ukrainian peoples thank their liberators, the brave German army. Heil Adolf Hitler!'

The people here are overjoyed, and it's a special piece of luck for us to be here, too. For we're fighting this battle not only against the world's poisoners, but in the case of the Ukraine we are liberating a people from an almost unbearable yoke. We are so proud, so happy!

Tuesday, 1st July 1941

Out of the sack at 2.00 a.m. Really, the saying 'no rest for the weary' applies to us. The attack is planned for 6.00, and after writing all my stuff I will just have time to wash and shave before our advance cars start off for rendezvous at 5.15.

It's a fabulous sight to watch our tanks move up into position —about 40 of them. At 7.30 we actually move off. At every point of attack we stop, anti-tank guns go into safety position, the men demount and the tanks crash through. At the second target we encounter strong tank opposition, but the Russians aren't up to our anti-tank guns nor to our tanks. When we move up later, the road and the ditches are jammed full of knocked-out enemy tanks.

There are hideous sights in the inside of the tanks—one man without a head, another sliced in two, the brains plastered over the walls—revolting. The Russian tanks aren't smaller than ours, you couldn't say that about a 72-ton tank; but in spite of this, their colossal machines are sure-fire targets for our tank-busting weapons. And our tanks are always quicker on the draw when shooting, even if it's only a split second. I've already counted 15 finished Russian tanks. And that's the way it goes on: we are constantly attacked by enemy tanks, they are constantly repulsed, till we reach the third objective.

Anti-tank guns and tanks move forward and secure positions. It takes some time till we can move up; then another tank battle. An enemy tank, in flames and without its crew, careers on by itself, rams one house and sticks in the middle of the second house. Others are standing at road crossings, their burning munition exploding all over the place and, though finished, dangerous.

We advance towards Sasov. Enemy tanks move in on us from all sides and are dispatched. We are supposed to break through from Kottov to Podkamien.

I receive the order to go back and fetch the reserves. We roar at 80 k.p.h. along the road. In front of a little village, a small road joins our main road from the left, and just as we are about 50 metres away, I notice at the last minute that a Russian tank has turned into the main road and is heading our way.

What can I do? We've no hand grenades with us, not even a carbine. And if the tank spots us, we're finished. The decision is made and carried through in a split second—drive right into the ditch. The machine turns over and we're in the ditch, lying flat on the ground. What we'd like to do is sink right through it. The grass is so cool, it's a good feeling at this moment. If only the tank won't get off the road and try to mash us to pieces. Henny! Karli! Lorli! Mother of Christ, what goes on in my head in these few seconds!

Slowly, carefully I raise my head above the protective ditch, and see the tank right in front of me; but it goes on.

We breathe a sigh of relief, and now we must go and inform the 7th Company at the eastern entrance of the village; you can see their vehicles clearly.

To try to get our vehicle back on the road is obviously impossible; it's got to stay where it is. For us to run in the ditch is not a good idea, either, because the Russian tank is sure to attack the 7th Company's lorries. Too dangerous. So: across the field.

We jump up and are about to run off when we see a Russian tank coming straight across the field towards us. No matter, back into the ditch and a mad dash for the 7th Company. The tank's shots are already whistling over our heads and we see them landing among the 7th Company's lorries. Dreadful roar now. Stumbling, crawling, we move on; far too slowly for me, for I want to get to the Company before the tank reaches the street. It's already coming near. Game's up. We run upright as fast as our legs can carry us. The two or three minutes we need are like hours, then we've made it to the Company, established in a park.

Everything there is utter chaos, everyone running round excitedly and not knowing what he ought to do. At last they move an anti-tank-gun into place, and it starts firing. In a few minutes the excitement is over and the tanks disappear. Thank the good Lord!

I bring the orders to the Company chief, then we grab a motor-cycle from the pool without asking anybody and tear off to the other companies. On my own initiative I also ask each of the chiefs to bring up the heavy weapons as well, and as quickly as they can. We can see the supply transports starting to move towards the front. We overtake them, ignoring the dust which is so thick that you can barely see. We drop the motor-cycle at the pool and go forward. After 1,000 metres the bullets start to sing past my head, and hunched over and then crawling along the ditch I reach my major and report that my mission has been successfully accomplished. Some of the units I notified are already there.

Now I learn that we almost suffered a bad defeat. The 8th Company penetrated the woods in front of us—about 100 metres—and received terrible infantry fire, partly from sharp-shooters in the trees and partly from marvellously camouflaged MGs. The Company lost 80 men. The chief is badly wounded. Those who got back told the most revolting stories you can possibly imagine. The wounded Kameraden were worked over by the Russians with gun barrels until they were dead. Many people saw this themselves.

Only the Russians can be that bestial. That's what they are anyway, beasts! No other people on earth, no other soldier in the whole wide world could act like such beasts. Unfortunately the German mentality is such that we won't even take revenge. I never saw any one of us touch a captured or wounded enemy soldier.

A new attack into the woods is set for 19.30. The 7th Company in front, followed at an interval by the 6th, supported by the tanks. The left-wing tanks have run out of ammunition, but that doesn't matter, they go along for moral support. At 19.00 the preparation begins—artillery, flak, mortars, MGs and every other kind of gun. It rains bullets in the woods. The tracers get stuck in the trees and underbrush, and there's a screaming roar as if the world was going under. It's revoltingly wonderful, terrific! You'd think every living thing in the woods must be extinguished.

At 19.30 on the dot we advance to the attack. The C.O., the aide-de-camp and I at the head of the 7th Company. It isn't the way it looks, and the I-A man of our battalion doesn't stay with his writing stuff behind the line of fire! My pen is now my gun and my ink my munition!

The basic principle of our commander is: the soldiers in the companies must know that their chiefs have no fear and are farther ahead in an attack than the company itself. I've only one fear: a battle in the woods is the worst possible thing there is for the one who's attacking. And what's more it'll be dark soon. Let's hope it ends well. And you, dear Henny, must cross your fingers for me so that no harm will come.

The tanks go with us up to the edge of the woods, which lie on a slope; they shoot into the woods a few times, then we've got to go on alone. Left one company, right the other, a few reserves on the road below. We three go on in front.

Nothing moves. Right from the beginning I have the impression that the enemy has withdrawn. A number of ruined tanks, probably hit by our artillery, lie on the road. All types: small, middle-sized, large—up to the 72-ton, that steel colossus. Some are burning, and in some the ammunition is still exploding. Some look as if they were intact, and I think their petrol must have run out.

We go through the woods. Still nothing moves. Across an open patch of ground. Still nothing. Then another wood, where we're supposed to halt at the east end, and the companies take up position. When we get to the east edge of the woods, it's already completely dark. Some shots crack. We return the fire. As we feel our way forward, we discover some Russians in a ditch. At once we hurl hand grenades at them and they disappear. We could nab two of them as prisoners. They tell us that there were only six of them.

The colonel came by and thanked the battalion for its showing in a day of severe fighting. We have hardly climbed into our car, tired from the day's events, and tired from hunger and thirst, and ready to sleep sitting up, when we get the order to march forward the next morning at 5.30. But not in today's direction. We're to go towards Tarnopol.

Wednesday, 2nd July 1941

Yesterday our unit alone destroyed 270 enemy tanks.

2ND JULY 1941

Towards noon we arrive in Tarnopol. Artillery, flak &c. are already installed in the hills round the town. At first the C.O., the aide-de-camp and I stand behind a house at the entrance to the town and watch the hits of the flak and artillery, who are covering the town with a mad carpet of explosions[1] before the attack.

You simply cannot imagine, Henny, what the concentrated fire of a reinforced motor battalion means; you think the world's at an end. The thunder and roar of the guns, the shots bursting as they land, the trails of tracers from the flak, the burning houses in the town, increased by the tracer shells[2] of our artillery. It's frightful—and beautiful. It would be quite understandable if the Russians in Tarnopol went out of their minds today.

The shellfire lets up and the company moves in, we at the head with our jeep. Left and right our men, a few tanks in advance, the C.O. standing up high in his car, calling encouraging words to each one of our incomparable soldiers, Zürn sitting on the left side, I on the right with my carbine in my lap. For safety's sake we fire a few rounds into the attic windows, but you can't tell if anyone is firing at us, so great is the noise. We get to about the middle of the town, and the C.O. calls a halt. The 6th Company hurriedly combs some of the streets, then we proceed. Next goal: railway bridge.

As our first men reach the bridge, we receive concentrated fire from the railway lines. We look up and see what's happening: a Russian railway armoured train with some 40 tanks mounted on railway trucks is about to steam off. The 7th Company, following us in vehicles, is sent to attack the station, while two heavy forward guns on self-propelled mountings drive on the bridge and start firing at the train. They go up, shoot at a tank-car, return, load up, and knock off the next one. Until the whole armoured train is shot to pieces and burning.

Then the men rush across the bridge one by one. We overtake

[1] 'Coordinated stonk' is the British *terminus technicus*. [H.C.R.L.]

[2] Prüller may mean the fire caused by normal shells: it has been doubted if incendiary shells were used as early as Tarnopol. [S.L.]

them at 100 km. tempo. Stuparits is on the bridge, firing his machine pistol, and a Russian two metres off gets Blank in the stomach and kills Stuparits. You can imagine how sorry I was about these two in particular; both of them were with me all during my time as recruit. It's always the best ones that get it.

Tarnopol is in our hands. We're to put the success to good use, so on, after the enemy! The two armoured scouting cars are sent ahead quickly on the advance road, the others trailing after them, and on we go with all the battalion vehicles, past an airport where the planes are still sitting ready to go on, and right through Smikovce.

We drive with our car ahead of the rest and experience a tank fight at first hand. Naturally we get out of the jeep and seek cover. Enemy artillery shells are landing all round us, enough to drive you mad.

At first as soon as you hear the shells screaming you lie flat on the ground without realizing that the shell has already gone past. Mostly, that is. There's another kind of screaming, though, which turns into an explosive bang right away. That means it hit near you. An old soldier knows this. So it really gets to be a matter of luck.

If the shell makes a direct hit, it's all over anyway. If it lands near you, or you hear the whining, hit the ground flat on your belly and hope a splinter doesn't get you. It's almost the same with tank guns. You do hear the thing firing, but the very next moment it lands and you almost don't hear any whining.

What do you think about at such a moment? As far as my orders allow me, I think of everything—of you, the children, home; of our parents, the future, my profession—everything spins round in your head at once, till all I think of is: if only I come through it alive.

To cap it all, it starts to rain. That's the worst, the most unpleasant thing that could happen! Afterwards, the C.O., the aide-de-camp, the driver and I sit in our car; the companies have dug themselves in. And so we wait for the morning, hoping the night won't bring any unpleasant surprises.

Thursday, 3rd July 1941

For today's advance we are assigned to the main body of troops. Yesterday and the day before that we were with the advance and did our share. The C.O.'s behaviour was particularly impressive. The way he pushed way in front, even ahead of the attacking company, standing straight up in his car, and sweeping the men with him, was terrific. Of course this produced a quicker and greater success.

The whole war takes place, more or less, on the road. Without securing the land lying to the right and left of the road, we move along and reach the appointed goals. How many Russians must be cruising round the country still! How many enemy tanks are off the road, hidden in protected positions, waiting for the right opportunity to rush up behind the troops and raise hell. Funny the way this war is being waged. But it's the only way. The success proves it.

At about 7.00 a.m. we march. It has begun to rain again, worse luck! We halt in front of Kamionka. To our left some flak guns go into position and cover the north. In a hollow we discover Russian cavalry, which the flak begins to fire at. You can see clearly through the binoculars the ruin that the flak is inflicting on the Russians. Horses and men lying about in wild disorder. You can see one of the Russians trying to raise himself up, and then his strength ebbs away and he collapses like a sack. It's frightful.

In the course of the afternoon we hear a shout near regimental battle headquarters: 'Enemy tanks! PAK to the front!' Our battalion is still pulling up, the 1st Battalion is way in front of Kamionka, and there isn't any PAK available. I grab a motorcycle and tear to the rear like a fire-engine to bring up some PAK. The road is cluttered up badly enough by stuff coming towards the front, and the disabled enemy tanks lying around make it even worse. It takes a long time for me to get back, grab the PAK platoon and go back with them. By that time a good three-quarters of an hour has gone by, and by the time I get to regimental headquarters, the PAK is no longer needed. A

Russian tank came from the north towards Kamionka, drove straight into battle headquarters with the turret open, the tank leader standing straight up, and about 10 Russian soldiers including women sitting on top of the tank. Each one had a pistol. They wanted to break through Kamionka to the east—suicide commando!

One of the Russians got the ordnance officer with a pistol shot. What good do our weapons do against such a huge tank? The thing went through Kamionka almost unscathed, and travelled right across the bridge going east before our flak picked him up. When we passed the demolished tank later, it was completely burned out. Some of the women, completely nude and roasted, were lying on and beside the tank. Awful. All along the whole road of approach you see Russians who have been mashed up by our lorries or tanks. If you look at one of them, you can't believe that it was ever a human being. An arm there, a head there, half a foot somewhere else, squashed brains, mashed ribs. Horrible.

We spend the night in the open, while the 1st Battalion builds a bridgehead at Volochisk which we're supposed to push through tomorrow. It's raining again. The rain is especially bad for us, an armoured division, because we can barely get through the bottomless mud of Russia. Up to now we've had the weather with us on all our campaigns. It's just this time that St. Peter seems to be on the Russian side.

Friday, 4th July 1941

When day breaks, we withdraw a bit because the ground we had encamped on can be seen by the Russians. It goes on raining uninterruptedly. Our motor-cycle driver finds a place in a house. I don't go on because of the stink inside. And when I just look at the people living there, I've had quite enough.

We spend the day here, and march at 19.00. We soon reach Odoczyska, where regimental battle headquarters has set up. A short conference and we're to fall in at once. I'm to determine the marching order of our group. I've filled my canteen with some alcohol. My constant companion. I prefer it to water, or tea or coffee, because it quenches the thirst better. Our colonel, too, always has a little bottle of vodka with him in one of his pockets. In many situations he takes a strengthening swig.

As evening falls, we reach Frydrychovka, leading the advance column of the 6th Company in our jeep. In the village, the C.O. halts. I go forward with the advance column and wait at the main village crossroads till he comes up. The heavy weapons have not caught up with us yet, so I have to go back and bring them up, especially the 8·8 flak. We come past a burning house; the whole corner of it could fall on our heads at any moment and ignite the munition. But nothing happens. Meanwhile the aide-de-camp has found a house to use as battle headquarters. The leader of the advance column, Lt. Bauer, with whom I went to the crossroads, has fallen, also Cpl. Stocken, an old member of the company.

We have heard the most horrible things about what the Russians are doing to our prisoners. We've got proof, too—it's not just the old atrocity tale—of what they did with the people in our 8th Company. On 1st July. And not only do we harm not a hair of a Russian's head, but our stupid men are so soft-hearted that they turn round the next minute and give these criminal riff-raff cigarettes! It's not people we're fighting against here, but simply animals.

Saturday, 5th July 1941

Among the Russian dead there are many asiatic faces, which look disgusting with their slit eyes. Dead women in uniform are lying around, too. These criminals stop at absolutely nothing.

We set up regimental battle headquarters in a former Russian military hospital. Awful the way it looks inside. In one room there are 10 dead Russians. Probably they died of their wounds. They tell us that we're going to be relieved by the SS. A few days of quiet would be nice, but after all the campaign has just begun. I think this is just wishful thinking.

It's a beautiful warm day. I don't sleep in the stink of the hospital, which is full, but lie down in the open. But I only managed to get ready when the advance orders for tomorrow arrived at 22.30. Just once I wish I could get a decent night's sleep. It's 2.00 before everything is ready. And at 6.00 we have to be up, ready to go at 8.00.

Sunday, 6th July 1941

At 8.00 we march, towards Proskurov. The 1st Battalion is the advance, we're with the main body today. The advance goes very slowly. Numerous obstacles keep slowing down our charge. You can't really call what we're on a road. It's better than this in the tiniest hamlet in Germany. And we're marching on a main road! The shoulders of the road are all muddy from the previous rain—you sink up to your knees—but in the middle of the road there's dust already. The covers of the vehicles are rolled back, the men sit in them in their helmets, carbines in their laps, each vehicle surrounded by an impenetrable cloud of dust.

Again we have to dismount and cross gigantic cornfields, never sure whether a whole battalion of Russians is right in front of us. Slowly we crawl along under the protection of mortar, artillery and heavy MGs.

When the men get near enough to the enemy holes, they go after them with cheers and hand grenades. Many of the Bolsheviks fall where they stand, though most of them try to flee and save themselves.

Monday, 7th July 1941

At 05.15 a big attack starts—our two companies with the 33rd Armoured Regiment as support. The ground leading up to the street, and the heights, are full of Russians, all dug in. It's the extension of the Stalin Line to the south.

Both companies are ready to 05.00; we drive with our jeep into position and the C.O. will lead the attack with his jeep. The ground round about is completely muddy from the rain. Slowly the tanks swing into position, the small, the middle-sized, the big ones. Everyone's in a fever of excitement, the way we always are before an attack. Our cheeks glowing, our eyes sparkling, our hearts beating faster, and our thoughts concentrated on one thing: to get them, to destroy them! By chance I remember that Lorli's birthday is today. But I haven't time to think about it long. Orders are given, the attack begins, the fight sweeps me into its course.

On the dot of 5.15 the steel giants move off: 140 of them! The Russians will soon be ready to shit. Unfortunately we don't get very far with our jeep. We get hopelessly stuck in a ditch and have to go on on foot. I took the precaution of bringing a bunch of dispatch riders with us; one of them carries the battalion flag that we take into every battle so that the C.O. is easier to locate. We hardly have time to reach the protection of a tall cornfield and to notice that our tanks have already reached the road, before heavy fire opens up from a forest to the left and from field positions ahead of us and from a barracks. We have to crawl into the cornfield. Only the pennant is held aloft, so that the companies following can find us, a disadvantage because the Russians continually shoot at our spot.

The tanks can't be called back any more because we haven't any contact with them. The C.O.'s jeep followed and wanted to go and fetch the tanks, but it got stuck again. As the driver was trying to decide how to get the jeep going again, he saw that the car was sitting over a hole out of which the barrel of an enemy trench mortar was protruding. He had to leave the jeep and saved himself only by galloping like a wild boar over the numerous Russian holes, each one full of Russians and well camouflaged. It's a nice story.

One company is already on the way to go round the woods and clean up the barracks. The C.O. wants to go with us—his little battle staff—through the woods and then to a little hill on the right, so as to be in the middle of both companies and have a bird's eye view of everything.

Machine pistol or carbine in readiness, we proceed through the woods. But there are only a few Russians there, and we mop them up after short opposition. Mayer carries the battle standard aloft, next to the C.O. As we approach the hill, they start firing at us. The bullets whistle over our heads, and it looks as if we are in the midst of the Russians' worst fire. Impossible to scale the hill; we haven't any MGs, only carbines, machine pistols and hand grenades. But just because it looks so impossible, we *must* go up. We must throw the Russians out.

We crawl along slowly, it would be mad to put your head up. The Russians are sitting in their well-camouflaged holes, and you can't see them. Finally some of our tanks return and seem to be looking for the C.O. I run back at once through the woods and get the tanks, so that they can help us smoking out the holes. We all breathe a sigh of relief when I arrive with the tanks and direct them towards the hill. They move up, we follow behind, shooting into the holes and throwing grenades into them. Fire is still pouring out of the holes, mostly without aim; the Russians don't dare stick their heads out of the holes. They simply stick their carbines out and press the trigger, or throw their grenades out without looking where to aim them.

The tanks drive over the holes, mash up and back a few times over each one, so that you'd think that the people in the holes had turned into soup; but no. They're still there, all over the place, shooting out of the holes and chucking grenades.

Lt. Kleine-Herzbruch drops next to me. Shot in the belly. Lt. Zürn stays the last few minutes with him. He dies in his arms without regaining consciousness.

We have to creep up to each hole, hurl a grenade inside, and then finish the Russians with pistols or rifles. No calls of surrender: the Russians prefer to be flattened out in their holes.

Here and there a steel helmet with two raised dirty hands appears. But we don't recognize any pardon after Schultes fell: as he was being bandaged, the Russians shot him again. And we all liked him so much; he was a grand boy. It isn't a fight any more that we're conducting now, it's a massacre!

It takes a long time for us to mop up, hole after hole, till there are no more shots.

We count the dead Russians. There are 135. We lost 11. By

one of the holes we stop a moment to regain our breath, and smoke a cigarette. We really earned that.

The C.O. wants to set up battle headquarters nearby. As we move off, we are attacked by H.E. shells from enemy anti-tank guns. I am walking between Lt. Kuhn and Lt. Zürn, they both drop. Lt. Kuhn with a stream of blood coming out of his mouth. In a second his head sinks to the left; he's dead. Lt. Zürn got a splinter in the upper part of his arm: thank God, a light wound, but still he has to go to the first-aid post.

I find the previous regimental battle headquarters next to the first-aid post. Oberleutnant Bauer is there, and I have to tell him what happened in the morning. Before I leave they tell me that Lt. Zürn has only a slight wound and will be back with us shortly.

On the way back I use the road ditch, and before I reach 3rd Company's position I have to stick my nose in the mud again. A roar and explosion as if the world were at an end, a blast of air flattens me on the ground and pieces of earth fall all over me.

A grenade has exploded, right next to me. I wait a few seconds. Then I feel all my bones from head to foot (which front soldier wouldn't have?), and when I see that nothing hurts and don't feel any warm trickles anywhere, I take off like a shot. I jump up and run as fast as my legs will carry me to battle headquarters. Good thing, too, because I made it in a pause between salvoes without knowing it.

As we lie in position and watch the Russians in front of us, standing around in a farmhouse, digging themselves in and getting reinforcements, we learn that our 1st Battalion, II/10[1] and the tanks are to attack again at 16.30.

And really, at exactly 16.30 the tanks with soldiers sitting on them attack. A tremendous shout of approval when we see that the Russians start to run as soon as they see our tanks coming! The Russian artillery has now stopped firing; probably they took off when they realized the danger. Perhaps they simply ran off and couldn't save their guns. The right thing now would be German bombers! They'd increase the confusion and make our job easier. But they can't be everywhere at once.

[1] 2nd Battaillon of Schützenregiment 10.

While we're cleaning up the cornfield we find some Russians still there who won't give up. There's no way out but to mow them down.

Tuesday, 8th July 1941

We spent the night in the open. We made ourselves dug-outs and covered them with sailcloth. After midnight it began to rain, and we couldn't stand it for much longer in those holes. Wet and shivering with the cold, we wait for morning. It brought us brilliant sunshine!

About 8.00 we marched off towards Proskurov. P. is better-known and a larger town in name only. Or rather according to the map. In fact there are the same huts as in other villages, only a few larger houses of stone, three storeys high, which are supposed to give the town a profile. And the few houses still standing are destroyed, burned out and collapsed.

On the main square, which we pass through, is a Lenin statue in the middle of a tired wire fence—you see this same wretched monument all over the place. The companies find quarters in the side streets. No one knows how long we're to stay here.

I set up our tent, because I can't work in the open. It begins to rain again. The C.O. has been designated Kommandant of Proskurov, and therefore there are all sorts of reports to make, recommendations for decorations, &c. The civilian population shows up in droves to have some impossible wish or other fulfilled. These rats! No wonder that everything is stolen and dragged off!

A woman asks for permission to occupy a flat whose owners have fled, leaving behind them what little possessions they had. The bitch doesn't really care about the flat at all; all she actually wants is to steal the little that remains in the hole.

We've never encountered people the like of this before!

I don't even know how late it is before I finally lie down on my trusty field cot. There's so much work, Henny, that I didn't even find time to write you. But that's my lot: to be up in front during battles, to write them up for the General and have paper work almost swamp me. And that's just what I like!

Friday, 11th July 1941

When I see even at this time of year how our vehicles, after it's rained a little, can barely make the grade, I just can't imagine how it will be in autumn when the rainy period really sets in. We're fighting in a solid mass of dirt. Outwardly and inwardly.

After Starakonstantinov we travel for the first time on a really first-rate asphalt road. Too bad it suddenly ends, as if chopped off, and turns into the usual bumpy, dusty road. It was only 35 km. long, but a relief all the same. At 3.00 in the morning we arrive in a village, Sudilkov, and halt there to find quarters. It's still pitch dark. We find a place in a garden. I stay right in my jeep and sleep sitting up, as I often do.

Saturday, 12th July 1941

At last it's a gorgeous summer day, with the only disadvantage that the enemy planes bomb the place. But as so often happens, all we hear is the whine of the bombs, their explosion, then after that we feel the air pressure—but nothing happens. The Russians are so stupid!

The school apparently harboured the Red Army, for there are various posters all over the place, referring to the war, with quotations of Stalin and Lenin hanging on red rags on the wall. Most of the windows are broken.

Sunday, 13th July 1941

It was cool, grey and rainy when we left at 6.30. An unfriendly morning. The advance goes slowly, with many pauses. We drive with the top down. When it started to rain heavily, the C.O. wouldn't stop. Water is now running off our seats, but the major has no pity. Thank God it stops an hour later.

In front of Polonje an infantry regiment turns in from the

right and marches with us on the road for a time. It is the former I.R. 134, a Viennese Regiment. Its badge shows the Steffel[1] on waves of the Danube. No wonder that my thoughts turned to my beloved Vienna, and that I had a great wave of homesickness for you and the children. That I thought of our beautiful buildings—of Schönbrunn Castle, the Prater, the Ring, the clean squares. And here we are, marching on the world's most impossible roads, driving these beasts before us! A tiny, dirty hovel: and a horse-drawn wagon of the German infantry with the Steffel on its sides. Two worlds . . . and the worse one shall be destroyed!

At 16.30—we're moving at top speed—12 Russian bombers appear over us. The best thing to do is to go right on, and we don't stop. I stand up a moment and see to the right of the road, about 500 metres away, an airbase. I suppose the Russians want to bomb the airbase and we'll be right in the middle of a rain of enemy bombs. I report this to the C.O. and the whole battalion stops. And really, the fliers drop a bit and the first bombs start to fall. But the Russians can't work at it for long: our own pursuit planes are soon there. It's a fabulous spectacle to see two bombers shot down and crash in flames; we greet this with loud cries of approval. Schober comes up from the rear, watches the drama, and as we're yelling with delight he says: 'Boy, it's just like a football game at the arena.'[2]

Tuesday, 15th July 1941

At 7.00 we march and take 4 hours to go 15 km. Then we rest till 12.30 and then on to right in front of Skvira, which was taken by our sister regiment (S/10). We drive the jeep into the town to Division C.O.

What's going on in the town is quite indescribable, you can't imagine the stealing, plundering, and robbing of the inhabitants!

[1] The affectionate Viennese diminutive for the Stefansdom, St. Stephen's Cathedral.

[2] In Viennese dialect (which I have translated very freely): 'Da gehts ja zua, wia am Spurtplotz.'

Everything that's not nailed down they drag away on their skinny backs—tables, chairs, beds, cupboards, sheets, crockery, curtains, whole flats, everything, the lot. . . .

At Division Headquarters we find an SS general in conference. On the advance route we're to be relieved by the SS. Although it looks as if we'll have peace and quiet for a few days, I'm sure that we'll be attacking tomorrow all the same. There's no thinking of rest: the road to victory, to destruction, to the complete annihilation of the Bolsheviks, is still a long one!

16th July 1941

My diary was lost the whole time from 5th July to now.[1] Just during the hardest battles. I wouldn't have had the time to put down all my impressions and experiences, I know, but I was very annoyed all the same. So I've put down all the purely external impressions in shortened form. At the outset:

Russia outdoes, in the poverty of its people, in the complete lack of civilization in its living standards, in the poor quality of clothing, everything we've ever seen. What particularly catches the eye, in every street, in every village we've come through, is that no people has ever stolen like this one! Not a shop goes unscathed. It's really worth seeing, the caravans of heavily laden sacks moving out of the shops. An empty shop is never left unplundered.

18th July 1941

At 14.30 Herr Oberst [Colonel], Count Sponeck came to our Regiment's C.O. and gave us the first Iron Crosses, 2nd Class, which have been given in the Russian campaign. I was the first to get it. Reason:

'Unteroffizier Prüller, as I.A. of the Battalion, through his quick personal action in the courageous fulfilment of his duties as

[1] We have filled in the gap from another diary which Prüller began on 6th July, discontinued after he recovered the present volume, and later used for other entries.

orderly, transmitted his orders so promptly to the designated posts that, when a Russian counter-attack threatened to succeed, he was able successfully to hinder the breakthrough. He undertook his assignment in the bravest fashion, despite the fact that he—driving a motor-cycle and sidecar—was attacked at short range on the street and on the land adjoining by (one in each case) Russian tanks. He has already been proposed for the Iron Cross, 2nd Class, on two previous occasions for similar bravery.'

In the evening I went to Transport for a short while and celebrated getting the Iron Cross with several bottles of champagne.

21st July 1941

Before we left yesterday a Russian prisoner arrived. But get a load of this, Henny: the fellow was 13, repeat *thirteen* years old. One doesn't know what to say any more. What a race!

Russia! A secretive veil lay even over the country of the czars. Is it the size of the country that does it? Is it the people? All you heard about through the continuous veil was about the oppression, the slavery. You didn't hear much about the poor, crushed people themselves. Only that they were poor, really poor in every sense of the word. Then came the World War, the separate peace, the Revolution, Bolshevism. And the veil was not lifted. On the contrary! You heard very little about Soviet Russia abroad, and nothing of abroad in the Soviet Union. The people were enclosed in a wall, books and periodicals from abroad forbidden, you couldn't travel. If foreign visitors came, they were shown model factories, model prisons, model houses, model farms, etc. . . . And now we have the reality: our path of advance led us across hundreds of miles. And it tore away the veil from the unknown Russia.

Peasant houses with straw roofs which look more like dog huts; a ragged, dirty, animal-like people; roads which are either messes of sand or rather, because it rains all the time, morasses of mud; the towns worse than the worst provincial backwoods nest at home. And despite all this, the land is so incredibly rich.

As far as the eye can see, wheat and cornfields without end. What's behind it all?

The prisoners give us the real reason: they flee to us before the whips of the Soviet state; even the political commissars, shooting wildly round themselves, can't stop them. Why? The paradise of the workers was nothing but lies and bluffing. The paradise of the workers was nothing but a conglomeration of hunger and misery, murder and mass imprisonments, slavery and torture. We shall crush them. So help us God!

24th July 1941

When I went to regiment headquarters this morning, the colonel was just explaining the general position in Russia. As far as we're concerned it's this: Here in the surrounding country we have six divisions in action. We are in the process of encircling the Russian troops in the Ukraine. Once more one or two Russian armies will have to capitulate in the next few days or be destroyed.

Up to now the Russians have lost way above 100 divisions. This means that the Russians have to all intents and purposes already lost the fight. They had to sacrifice their best troops in the border battles at Byalistok and Minsk; their losses in materials and weapons and machines are gigantic and irreplaceable. All they can send into battle now are masses of people, barely equipped and with hardly any weapons. It is clear that those won't be able to offer much, if any, resistance.

I reckon that the Russian campaign will be over by the middle of September.

27th July 1941

Yesterday it began to rain and it hasn't stopped yet. It's enough to make you desperate. No one thought about it till someone mentioned it: today is Sunday! It's amazing how little it matters. One loses almost completely any sense of time. In the transmitter car next to my tent they've turned on the wireless.

They are just playing 'Hörst Du mein heimliches Rufen'.[1] My God! how wonderful this Sunday morning at home would be. What am I saying, *this* one? No, *every* one! We should have had more time between Greece and our next tour of duty—at least more than those four days we managed to steal. Then we wouldn't be homesick so soon.

28th July 1941

At 8.15 I wake up, in time to find Zürn there with the order that the Battalion must fall in at once and advance to Lissjanka. In the night it didn't rain for a change, and still isn't, so it may be possible for us to get the vehicles moving.

The condition of the roads in Russia is simply indescribable. If we were astounded and annoyed about the roads in the Balkans, they're far worse here. Altogether I would recommend that every German communist be dragged to Russia, so that he could see what the worker's paradise looks like. I haven't found anything to like here except for one point: on the so-called roads they have put up signs for curves which show which way the curve will go. I think that's better than our 'S' signs.

We advance to Smiltschenzy and wait for the Battalion there. The local inhabitants bring us eggs, milk, apples and cherries, and won't take a penny for them. They come with Russian maps and want to know how far the German Wehrmacht has penetrated. None of them speaks German, but 'Geben Sie mir eine Zigarette'—that they can say.

Today I finally had a chance to find out about what a Russian worker earns. Take a baker's apprentice, for example. He gets 250 to 300 roubles a *month* here. Typical prices here are: haircut, 4 roubles; one stick of shaving-soap, 4 roubles; a pair of trousers —such as would cost 6 Reichsmark at home—100 roubles. And so on.

Our goal is to be Swenigorotka. I have the feeling that the enemy have left the place, or at least that there aren't very many of them there.

[1] 'Do you hear my secret call?'—a popular song.

31st July 1941

There is a difference between this diary and the ones I kept in Poland, France and Greece. In my Poland notes, the young soldier, not yet battle-tested, is speaking; he has yet to endure the test of fire. Apart from that, I was No. 1 of a machine-gun team and all I had to do was to watch out for my MG. If in the course of the advance we lay in a field, or waited on the road, I could at once put down on paper all my thoughts, my hopes, my wants and requests for you; and I could describe the single phases of the battles I experienced.

Now there has been a significant change: I've been placed in a position where I can see what's going on at the battalion, often the regimental, level. You will surely understand that, though before all my thoughts were of you, now I haven't time to get down all the battle impressions. Another factor is that I have only very little time now for my own actions. The diaries, though, are still written only for you, mainly to let you know what I am seeing, doing and thinking in case something happens to me.

After proceeding for 15 km., I discover that my dispatch case together with its entire contents must have fallen off the motorcycle somewhere along the line. I'm most sorry of all about the diary.

I turn round, intending to trace my way back. Lt. Zürn comes up, and I tell him what happened. He remembers someone from the 10th Company (the end of our column) reading a book which looks like my diary. I go back along the impossible road all the way to the 10th Company, and find that—miracle of miracles!—the noncom has my case. You can imagine how happy I was. I wouldn't have had it in me to begin a new diary again.

Again I go along the rotten road of advance, past our whole column, to Tishkovka. There the 10th Armoured has captured a batch of prisoners, some women among them, some of whom are wounded. They could really find something better to do than going to war! Painted and powdered they are, not at all looking as if they were part of a fighting front. Perhaps some of them are in fact there only to satisfy the lusts of the Bolshevik hordes, who have written sexual freedom on their flag anyway.

In Tishkovka, at the edge of town, is our battalion battle headquarters. The companies are already in position. Our job is to nab the encircled Russians—the circle is closing in on them all the time.

I have often noted something which I don't want to miss putting down. The windows in all the houses—or rather huts—are built solid into the walls so you can't open them. The Russians have to bring in the fresh air in their rucksacks, as far as they feel any need of it.

It's interesting to watch the sunflower fields. When the sun sets in the evening, the flowers point westwards. In the morning they are all pointing eastwards and follow the sun the whole day.

You simply cannot imagine what a happy feeling it is to see such a country, Henny! As far as the eye can see: fields, corn, wheat, field after field. This great country we are capturing for our children. This earth! This wealth! It's simply wonderful!

4th August 1941

Yesterday it rained cats-and-dogs several times. In the evening, we got the orders for today's attack. On our right a reinforced battalion from the 11th Division will go with us. Towards Ternovka. Henny, cross your fingers that it'll be all right, and that the Russians won't be all too strong.

We reach Ternovka at 19.00. It was a terrible day for us, just like that four weeks ago on the hills above Krzywacynce. But the result has been tremendous. Our Battalion all by itself captured 3,000 prisoners. The booty in vehicles, guns and other stuff is so enormous that we don't even know exactly how much it is.

At 8.15 a.m. we began the attack. Before we reached our goal, the 7th Company, moving along the road on the right, received murderous fire. The men of a PAK which had gone ahead had to demount and got mixed up in the fight as well. We in our jeep were with the 6th Company, on the left-hand side of the road, and pulled up on a rise. Battle headquarters was to the left behind a hill. You could barely show yourself without a bullet whistling over your head. The Russians were well dug into the corn and sunflower fields and couldn't be reached. The tanks were unfortunately way up ahead and had to be pulled back. A flak unit moved forward to root out the Russians. Everything we've got—light artillery, heavy machine-guns, etc.—was put into action. To no avail.

I was standing behind a pile of hay, trying to see where the Russians were. No good. I had barely left the place and gone to the other side of the street, when Captain Sartorius, who was where I had been, fell with a shot through his head. Perhaps it would have got me if I'd stayed there. Enemy fire from the right got steadily worse, when from the left, about 2,000 metres away, a Russian column moved towards us. When Sartorius and I saw them an hour ago, we had thought they had been our 10th Armoured! In great haste we moved most of our guns to the left and started firing in that direction.

I had to go and tell the flak, which was farther up ahead, so that they could train their 8·8 batteries on them. The bullets were all around me when I ran up and back, but nothing happened. Our first shots started landing over there, and immediately some of the vehicles started to burn, horses began running round, riderless, and the first Russians came across, hands over their heads. It was fabulous! Meanwhile some of our tanks came back from up ahead, crossing right into the fields to the right of the road. There, too, some Russians appeared and gave themselves up. But when they saw the tanks, many of them stayed in their holes and even threw hand grenades at the tanks. It wasn't until our men attacked between the tanks that most of the Russians popped out.

Before this the 6th Company went over and beyond the hill and attacked there. There wasn't much going on, though; but after a few minutes it was reported that Wimmer fell. Such a fine man! I'm so sorry for his wife, especially since she's going to have a baby in October. And the funny thing is, Wimmer was quite sure nothing would happen to him. Such a bullet gets there in a hurry, and then . . . you're finished.

The attack went on smoothly, and one Russian after another came out of the fields and surrendered. That's what we like. We drove all the time between the men, in front of the men, between the tanks, and even that wasn't enough for the C.O.: we had to go in front of the tanks! We often had to dismount because of the rain of bullets, but luck was with us.

On the last rise before our final goal—Ternovka—we halted once again: our commanding general was there. Then we're off, the men sitting on the tanks. When we got across the hill, we received enemy artillery fire and had to seek cover. But the view in front of us! Russian vehicles as far as you could see, positively without number! Through my stereo-telescope I saw quite clearly how a Russian column, at their head a tank, was pulling out of Ternovka. The C.O. ordered me to go at once and inform the C.O. of the 33rd Armoured. While I was looking for him, Schober fell in the very place I had been standing. Kismet?

An enemy grenade exploded 6 metres away from battle headquarters; 2 motor-cycle drivers were wounded with the splinters, and Schober got a splinter under his left eye and right through his head. He was dead on the spot. It's curious. Isn't luck really on my side?

Towards evening we force our way into Ternovka. I rush ahead and requisition a first-rate car for myself, to work in. The place is still full of Russians, and prisoners tell us that there are supposedly two generals in the place. At 22.00 I lie down, dog tired, on some straw. It was a terrible day. But again luck was with me. How long will it last?

6th August 1941

The wildest rumours are going round again. Some say we're to go to Roumania, others say we shall winter here, still another says we're to go home. It wouldn't be such a mistake for us to go home, for we've about 350 losses in the Battalion. August 4th alone cost us 14 dead, 47 wounded, 2 missing, 1 officer dead and 3 wounded.

At 21.00 the advance order came through that we're to be pulled out of here. Supposedly five days of rest first. That would be fine!

10th August 1941

I had all my dirty linen washed. The people here positively refused to take any money. So I give them a handful of cigarettes. The husband of the woman who did my washing was sent to Siberia during the mass arrests in 1937. She hasn't any idea where he is—four years no news of him. That's Soviet Russia for you!

At 22.00 we get tomorrow's orders: we're to be moved farther east.

11th August 1941

We leave at 8.15. It's marvellous weather again, although the wind fills our traps with a terrible lot of dust. It appears that the roads get better the farther eastwards you go; but they are still beneath criticism and cannot be put in the same category as any other European roads; still, better than at first.

At 11.30 we arrive at Noaya Praga. It's supposed to be a little city. Our dirtiest, most God-forgotten industrial centre—in case we have anything like it at all—is a little jewel compared to Noaya Praga. I simply can't imagine how the Russians could stand the Bolshevist régime for a quarter of a century. Wherever you look you see the worst sort of decay.

12th August 1941

Last night we sat round a table which we'd commandeered, our chairs drawn up close, and exchanged opinions about the future situation in Russia. Reischitz, the C.O.'s driver, Stiegler, Lt. Oktabetz's driver and I. In the midst of our war discussions, our thoughts switched to home, the way they always do in a quiet minute.

What will you be doing? And the children? And your mother? How are you all? What will you be thinking of our gigantic advances, of our incomparable victories?

Good God! How wonderful it would be to be at home again! To be in peace and quiet again. No thoughts about the war, or death and destruction, or the advance, the attack, the enemy artillery and rifle fire, or dead and wounded. No! To have none of that, just quiet. To sit comfortably on the sofa with a glass of beer and a cigarette and listen to music . . . or to you playing the piano . . . or to go with you to the theatre . . . or to play with the children . . . or just to be somewhere talking . . . or to be sleeping in a real, white, soft bed . . . or to be sitting at a table, properly set, eating with knives and forks . . . or to be reading a good book . . . or . . . or . . .

This week, says R.,[1] we'll cross the Dnieper; but S.[1] doesn't think so. What a shame about Schober, that capital fellow we lost on the 4th. Our talk goes on about this and that.

Slowly it gets dark. The sky above us is deep blue, a starry heaven. A cool, light wind blows gently. The Kameraden are mostly in their tents or vehicles and the majority are asleep. Only our dispatch riders and that indestructible Pischek are sitting together in a corner of the park. They are digging away in the past, the present, and the future.

The C.O. is playing cards with his cronies—'Doppelkopf', a game which gets on our nerves.

In the midst of all these thoughts, in this nocturnal silence, suddenly music falls on our ear. Wonderful music. A balalaika is playing. A guitar. It's not a gramophone, it's not the wireless. No: Ukrainians have come to us, they sit down in the park and play us their songs. We listen to them for hours, as they play and sing of their home. Because we fancy that they could almost be Viennese songs. Isn't that piece dedicated to the Kahlenberg; isn't that one about the Danube; and that one about the Steffl? or the Lichtenthal? But no, the ever quicker tones of the bala-

[1] Reischitz; Stiegler.

laika, often a crazy pace, reminds us that we are deep in Russia, that we are hearing Russian songs.

We go on listening—a long time. Till a very slow, intimate folk song is played, always getting softer and softer, and we sleep. And our hearts are so heavy.

13th August 1941

'Unteroffizier Prüller, it's 2.30 in the morning!' That's how I was woken up—the first man in the Battalion. I had gone to sleep at 12.00.

I rub my eyes, but they don't want to stay open. Two and a half hours' sleep is not very much. But it'll have to do. A quick look out of the car: it's not raining. Fine. A wash in rain-water, on with the clothes, then tea and bread and butter which is ready in spite of the early hour, and then as far as I'm concerned we can go.

It becomes clear that my early rising was no use, for the C.O. lies in his sack a quarter of an hour after having been wakened. It's not the first time, either. Meanwhile it's light outside. At 4.15 we leave. When we get to regimental battle headquarters, there's nothing there; they've moved across the Ingulets River.

To see the advance roll along is a grand sight—left and right the companies of the 1st Battalion, deeply echeloned, then the artillery and 60 tanks way up ahead. It's 6.15. There's quite a nip in the air, even with a rubber greatcoat, but the sun appears slowly and it's soon a lovely day. The attack goes very smoothly, despite enemy pressure against onc flank: the tanks really are very useful.

Zürn discovers a Russian 500 metres away beside a haystack. I drive there with Pischek, my machine pistol in my hand, fall off the machine, and accidentally fire a shot; when we get to the haystack the Russian is found to be wounded. Did my accidental shot get him?

Mail is supposed to arrive today. I hope there's something for me, too: a letter, or even better, cigarettes.

We proceed for the most part through fields, wheat, potato

and beet fields, etc. Hope our vehicles can hold out. As we are driving the C.O.'s car, I catch sight of a large number of Russians behind the opposite hill. We are way up front with the advance scouting units. Before we can discuss what to do, a civilian car drives towards us. Two hundred metres away it stops. Russians inside. We wave at them with pieces of white cloth to try to get them to surrender. One man gets out of the car, gets in, and then gets out again. It looks as if he wants to prepare a little flag, but unhappily our PAK shoots twice at the car, and the man runs off. We all had the definite impression that the Russians wanted to give themselves up, but now that's been fouled up. It was in fact a mean trick, though unintentional, for us to wave a white cloth at them and then to shoot. But it wasn't anybody's fault. There will always be characters with nervous trigger-fingers.

What good is it going to do us now when we get out the big map and wave the white reverse side to the Russians? They won't come any more. In short, I decided to take some men with me and go and get 'em.

We go past the car. A woman is at the wheel, and our PAK shot so accurately that half her face is missing. Before we reach a hollow which separates us from the Russians, I see another Russian car driving down the road towards us. I run as fast as I can with a white cloth to the road. The car stops about 50 metres away: two officers are sitting inside, wave our offer away, turn the car round and tear off. I don't shoot at them, otherwise we'll never get them to come over.

We go on a few hundred metres towards the hollow. Suddenly the Russians throw two rounds of MG fire at us. In a second we're on our bellies. Apparently they don't want to give up after all, even though they're being pressed on the other side, too. Or perhaps it's their revenge for the PAK shots. Anyway, we return and leave the Russians to our artillery and heavy machine-guns. . . .

14th August 1941

We are again driving through open country and ploughed

fields, our C.O.'s car right in the middle of the tanks. People stand curiously in front of their houses. They probably can't take it in that German tanks are already here, and at this early hour of the day, too.

At 7.00 a.m. we are in front of Krivoi Rog, which is supposed to be the eighth largest city in Russia (?). Some civilians we've grabbed tell us that the Russians left the city during the night. A long column is just rolling out of the city towards the east, but we don't bother about them because we want to occupy the city.

As we hear a number of explosions within, the C.O. decides (after getting the Regiment C.O.'s approval) to take the city without any previous artillery preparation, so as to save what can be saved. The tanks go ahead, we in the middle, followed by the companies, sitting on vehicles.

The city makes a good impression and is intact. A row of chimneys on the city outskirts and many factories would seem to suggest a great deal of industry. In the suburbs we are greeted with flowers, waving of hands, 'Heil!' and 'Hurrah'. Isn't it a crazy world? In the city itself we are greeted in a very friendly way by the population. Only a few shots from partisans disturb the good reception.

The main part of the city has paved streets—the first time we've ever seen anything like this in our dear Russia! Also some large houses, hotels, department stores, etc. But we've no time now; first we've got to take possession of the bridge across the Ingulets River and the railway bridges. One concrete bridge was all ready to be blown up, and fuses burning all over the place, but unfortunately for the Russians we arrive too soon, for Lt. Frankenfeld of the 6th Company is already ripping away the fuses.

We make our battle headquarters on the main street in a large hotel. Everything is empty when I go through it; only a civilian is busily taking off all the Stalin, Voroshilov, etc., pictures from the walls and destroying them.

The civilians are dragging off huge bundles of plundered goods; it was so bad that we got an interpreter to forbid them doing it. I don't think it will do much good. One of the people from the jail (whom the Russians set free) is wandering through the streets, drunk and yelling. I have him arrested, but in the afternoon he's there again, and in the evening, when he gets too uproarious, he's shot.

With pride and joy we hear in the evening a special announcement on the wireless about our capture of the city. Even if there wasn't any real trouble in taking it, still we're very pleased that it was we who did it. We had one dead and 4 wounded: no losses at all compared to the importance of the gain.

15th August 1941

In the course of the morning we take up safety positions on the south-east side of the city, where there are three large factories. We find a park there—and just as if the Russians were waiting for it, we get an air raid.

Next to us is a little pond. A nice opportunity for us to wash and bathe properly. It's curious to see the Russian women shamelessly undressing in front of us and wandering round naked. Some of them look quite appetizing, especially their breasts. . . . Most of us would be quite willing to . . . but then again you see the old dirty ones and you want to go and vomit. They've got no morals here! Revolting!

17th August 1941

We wanted to get inside Zaporozhe today, the first town across the Dnieper. It was 190 km. away. What we pulled off today makes the Wild West look silly: driving full tilt into marching Russian columns, from straight on, from the side, firing a few MG rounds at the Russians to scare them and then pulling out white cloths and waving them; we charged into Russian soldiers who were in the process of dragging thousands of agricultural machines across the Dnieper, disarmed them and whisked on towards the Dnieper; we tore past soldiers, civilians, past women and children..

We barely dismounted, just waved our white cloths at 'em, and collected hundreds and hundreds of prisoners. The booty in weapons, machines, horse-drawn lorries and horses is simply vast. We were possessed by one thought alone during this mad rush forward: to secure the bridge over the Dnieper at Saporoschje. We left untouched many enemy columns to the right and left of us; just didn't bother about them.

Towards evening, we hit quite a decent road, but about 20 km. in front of the Dnieper we met with strong resistance. Too bad that it was getting dark and we had to stop and go into position for the night.

18th August 1941

I had the first decent night's sleep in three days. Up to yesterday evening I'd had a total of 3½ hours. In the morning enemy trench mortars begin to firc at us, and we suffered some losses. The more passively we react to it, however, the worse our losses are, because the Russian mortar can't be silenced. And the way we always feel, there's only one answer in this situation, too: attack.

We move up about one km., capture several prisoners, but stop in front of an anti-tank trench. Short pause for rest, then orders to the heavy guns and the attack is set: for 10.45. On the dot it begins, too. Those Russians we can spot are either hauled out of their fox-holes, or they come by themselves, or we mow them down. Most of the Russians, in their dirt-brown summer uniforms, come of their own accord. They go past us at a trot, deathly fear on each one of their faces. They all try, with gestures, to find out where that crazy rain of bullets raining down on them came from. They just can't stop us, the Russians, never! We see it again and again.

Again fate was kind, dear Henny, and saved me for you and the children! Let us thank God for it!

Slowly we move into the village and establish battle headquarters in the barracks there.

The Russians are still shooting at us sporadically. Then they begin to lob trench mortars at us, and hit the house that we are standing behind three times. Because it's mortar fire, it's not so bad: mortars burst at the slightest touch. A few remains of the roof land on our heads. The sporadic fire increases, mainly where the 8th Company is. There the Russians make a counter-attack, the Company gets nervous and withdraws.

At the entrance to the village there are still a few of our tanks. I get them. They all have their turrets shut, and it takes me quite a time to make myself understood. Then I sit on the top of one of them; the iron is so boiling hot from the sun that I can barely stand it. The turret is still screwed down, and so it takes a time for me to guide the tank towards the right direction. But I finally succeed.

The tanks and two flak instalments enable us to push the enemy back. It wasn't very pleasant, especially for me, sitting on the tank with no cover; but the main thing is, it succeeded.

Since we want at all costs to reach Zaporozhe today, it's obvious that we shall have to attack again. It's set for 17.00, and I hope it's the last one today. The Russians go on shooting at us with their mortars, then with artillery, then with MGs and rifles. We move out, past the last houses, and then comes the railway, followed by a large anti-tank ditch and behind that a park. Behind all this the goal lies: the Dnieper with its enormous dam, the largest in Europe, and farther south, the railway bridge.

Under cover of tank fire we push into the park. There are numerous fox-holes, most of which were just being dug before we attacked. They show that the Russians must have thrown up their defence works here in a terrible hurry. And as we leave the park, we see the grey strip which is the Dnieper (if it were only the Danube!), the railway bridge, the dam. Meanwhile the light has begun to fail, so that it's out of the question for us to occupy the dam or go across it. While our gathering companies rendezvous, what each of us has been expecting—and in our innermost hearts hoping for—happens: with an enormous roar part of the dam is blown sky-high. For us the path across the Dnieper is cut off. Thank God! too, is what most of us are thinking.

20th August 1941

At 08.00 we roll into Tschumaki. The whole Battalion and also regiment headquarters take up positions in the town. We barely get settled when orders come that we shall probably march on today. We sit around the whole day and wait for further orders, which don't want to come.

In the evening I lie down in the straw together with several drivers. It's a wonderful, mild evening. The heavens are full of stars, and the news boys have turned on the wireless and filled the air with music.

Isn't it understandable that before we go to sleep the idea of going home seems to us very rosy? Isn't it obvious to be home-sick for you and the children? Life could be so wonderful, so precious. The war isn't exactly the opposite, but we've simply had too little leave so far. That's the whole point. And besides, we've four campaigns behind us. Who can blame us for dreaming of home, of peace and quiet?

But despite this: if orders come tomorrow to attack, we shall carry them out with our usual enthusiasm, with our old battle spirit, with our usual courage. That's the miracle of the German soldier!

25th August 1941

At 12.05 we are the first to reach the bridge, and proudly report this to the Regiment. A little later the 60th Infantry Division marches into the city [Dnepropetrovsk] in perfect formation, singing a song as they do. The city makes a fine impression, some new and tall houses, mostly institutes or schools; probably the place has trams, too.

We establish battle headquarters in a villa near the bridge, but since we are constantly under enemy fire, we move near the regimental battle headquarters at the other end of the city.

Now we've given them our helping hand, and hope that we shall now have our well-earned rest. But no. We aren't pulled out, but have to go and secure the west bank of the Dnieper.

28th August 1941

We had to change quarters several times. Enemy artillery follows us, it would appear. In the night a large number of enemy bombers come and work over the city. Are they perhaps English? That dirty pack, who have now allied themselves with the Russians, though two months ago they were yakking away in solemn tones against the Bolsheviks!

The weather is wonderful. Almost too hot. The food is simply terrific. Pork every day. I'm eating for three; as far as the meat goes, for five. And since I became a *Feldwebel* [Sergeant] yesterday, to take effect retroactively as from 1st August, I'm entirely satisfied for the next few days.

Some wonder at my advancement, for I've not even three full years behind me, and others get it only after five or more years. But the main thing is that the C.O. is satisfied with me. Lt. Zürn isn't wild about it because he wanted me to re-enlist for a longer period beforehand;[1] but I can always do that if the war really goes on for longer. And finally, it's you who get my pay now, and that will be a good bit more than the previous extra family allowance; and we can certainly use that.

1st September 1941

Today, on the first day of the third war year, all the hopes of going home have definitely gone down the drain: or of our going to Krivoi Rog, the rest centre, though we'd even sent our quartermaster ahead there—that's off too. We are to stay for the time being as safety units on the other side of the Dnieper. I think that everything with wheels will reach the Caucasus.

We enter the third war year in the firm belief and with the unshakeable will to win. Let us hope it will be the last. We are sure, however, that it will by far top the two previous ones in honourable victories and successes. May the Lord be gracious to me in His blessings this coming year; for then it will end well.

[1] Enlistment was generally for six or twelve years; apparently Zürn wanted Prüller to re-enlist for the full twelve.

God's will be done! Forward to new deeds! Long live our dearly beloved Führer!

2nd September 1941

When I found my vehicle again in Sviskije, I could scarcely believe that we had managed to survive such a hard day. We've had to change our positions several times during the last six days on account of enemy fire; but today was the worst. It started, the fireworks, in the morning. I was working on the car when the first grenades landed in the courtyard in front of our house; some crashed down behind my car; the little hut next to me was then set on fire by another. I had the car driven behind the house then. In the house itself, which must have been a technical school or something like it, the drivers' pool, some radio technicians and telephone operators, the C.O.'s aide-de-camp and some of my drivers were living. The rest of the staff had already moved out, to Surskije.

The artillery fire was getting steadily worse, and large roars marked the explosions landing all round us. The windows were soon shattered—there weren't very many left anyway—and dust and smoke poured in through the holes; pretty soon the whole countryside was rolling in through the windows. But we didn't mind that so much. What really infuriated us and finished us, was when we entered the place and found the Russian artillery observer[1] lying next to the door. Several splinters had got him. Dead.

At noon there was a little pause, but as I was getting ready to write the orders for us to relieve the motor-cycle units of the Hermann Göring Battalion, the fire started off again. Apparently aimed right at us. The C.O. ordered us all to go into the cellar. And there luck was with us, too: there were two cellars, and in the one we weren't using, two shells landed, reducing it to a complete ruin.

During this period, the most incredible thing of all occurred.

[1] He had crawled through the lines with his portable transmitter and had been directing the Russian fire.

Some of our people—among them the indestructible Pischek—were standing on the stairs just when a shell exploded in the ground floor of the south-east side of the house, in the room next to the stairs. The cross-beams and the roof tiles flew round, burying 'Pepi' [Pischek] under a pile of rubbish. When we dragged him out, he was unconscious. Heart and pulse were all right, though. I wanted to take him to the main dressing-station myself, and drove the car in front of the door, when our Chief Surgeon came and sent for the ambulance for him. One hour later Pischek died at the first-aid station. One of our best, bravest and most capable soldiers is no longer with us. I can scarcely believe it!

The Russian artillery stops for a bit. We all prepare to go; the C.O.'s and aide-de-camp's batmen clear the stuff into his vehicle, when another shell lands in the courtyard. Our interpreter, a Russian Jew we've had with us for some time, is the only one in the courtyard. Nothing happens to *him*.

A shell landed in the afternoon on the corner of the house, right over my vehicle. The walls fell on top of the car roof, and it now looks like a lumber mill. I hope the car can be used, or rather repaired.

4th September 1941

Today I spoke to Oberleutnant Eichert, C.O. of the 6th Company. I'm supposed to go back to my old Company; they need me there urgently. I shall go with the greatest of pleasure. The C.O. here wants to get rid of me, I want to go, and so everybody will be happy. You don't need to worry, my dearest Henny, it can't be more dangerous in the Company than it is here where I am now, with the Battalion. On the contrary. In the Company I'm only in front when the Company goes into action, while here I'm out front every time the Battalion goes into action. All my old friends from the Company who are still here are delighted at my coming move.

5th September 1941

Today I drove not with the C.O.'s tub, but with our travelling office-lorry. At 15.00 we arrived, at the tail-end of the column, in Pokrovskoye. Here there's electric light and running water. We are put up in a school. A stay here of four or five days, during which time all the vehicles are to be put in order.

7th September 1941

When meals are dished out in our field-mess, a line of women and children is always standing there to get their pots filled. Our 2nd cook, a giant in height and girth of belly, but with a heart of a small child, always fills the people's pots full.

'So long as we can do it, and as much as you can eat,' is what he always says, and always adds a ladle for good measure. The Russians stand at the kitchen with tears in their eyes. They just can't believe that we not only don't hurt them, but that we give them food on top of it all. Oh yes, we German barbarians!

10th September 1941

The day before yesterday I had my farewell from Staff. A small circle. It went on till 4.00 a.m. Today I bade farewell officially and for the last time. I went to Staff in 1940 gladly and willingly, and as gladly as I came then, I go now. It wasn't up to me. I thanked Oberfeldwebel Marakovits officially: it was his doing that I'm what I am today. Then I bade farewell to the C.O. and transferred at noon back to the Company.

Only a few of my friends are still here. Ninety per cent are new people. I'm C.H.Q. leader and thus constantly with the C.O. I don't go into the orderly-room any more; I've had enough of that.

Thursday, 11th September 1941

When our Division gets home for good, we've a big plan. We

want to erect a beautiful big monument in honour of our dead on the outskirts of Vienna. A constant and thankful reminder of these heroes, and a memorial for those dear to them. For the relatives at home the earth of all the larger battlefields is to be collected in urns, and the names of our dead are to be inscribed in memorial books, separated into the various theatres of war. The money for the building is to be raised by all the Division units, and from our own private money. Isn't this a splendid idea on the part of our Division C.O.?[1]

At 16.30 we marched off on schedule, but didn't get far—scarcely 20 km. No lasting halts. Then it began to rain cats-and-dogs. We stood there, then went on a few miles, then stood still again—the whole night. We slept sitting up in the vehicles.

There was one single comfort: we still heard the Belgrade 'Wachtposten'.[2] The song has really won the hearts of us soldiers. Despite the pouring rain, we all stood round the transmitter car and listened to the music, which flows so easily into one's ear. And the lovely words! Personally I've been listening to it every day for a fortnight. I've got to hear it, otherwise I'm not wholly myself.

Friday, 12th September 1941

After a few more stops and starts we finally arrive at Petrovo to spend the night. It's 12.15 a.m. and it's taken us 20 hours to go 60 kilometres! It's almost unbelievable!

We take up quarters in a house but don't go in yet because it's not certain whether we're to go on in the evening or not. When the orders come through that we shall apparently move on in the early morning, we set up night quarters in the stinking hole. As in all peasant houses, there's no window that you can

[1] The money, deposited in an account with the Postsparkasse, disappeared after the war, and a plaque to honour those who had fallen was put up in a Viennese church (Stiftskirche).

[2] A famous programme given by the German Army Radio from Belgrade, the 'theme tune' of which was 'Lili Marlene', the song to which Prüller refers. Sometimes he refers to it only by the name of the programme, the Belgrade 'sentry'.

open here either. We break two small window panes, which will probably be described as barbarous. Imagine people being able to *stand* it!

On the wall hangs a map of Russia. That it hangs upside down they don't even know. After all, it's supposed to show their education and their interest in the great Soviet empire. Some pictures, coloured, with glittering junk, are what you see in every house. Perhaps it's the custom; is this supposed to represent enthusiasm for the Fine Arts?

There is no electric light, no toilet, no running water, etc.—but there's a loudspeaker. There is one wireless apparatus for the whole village, and from it everyone hears the blessings of their paradise. I think, however, that the real reason is that the people aren't supposed to listen to foreign broadcasts.

At every step you find new proofs that it's foolish people living here. If I had a choice they would have to drag me to Russia with wild horses, I find the place so revolting.

Monday, 15th September 1941

In the afternoon one of Oberleutnant Eichert's good friends from the 16th Armoured Division came on a visit and explained the overall situation: Guderian's armoured units—coming from the north—and Kleist's—coming from the south—have met at Lubjan, some 30 km. northwards of here. Thereby the enemy is trapped way behind his own lines near Kiev. Fifty Russian divisions must face capitulation or destruction! The C. in C. Marshal Budjenni is with them!

A feint manœuvre has succeeded brilliantly. The Russians were expecting the tank groups to cross the Dnieper at Zaporozhe or Dnepropetrovsk; but the main body crossed at Kremenchug, a few of them going eastwards, but most of them rushing to the north. And in that way we connected with Guderian. Of course now we aren't going to wait for the Russians to come but will close up the circle. It was another colossal performance on Guderian's part, even if he did work with amphibious tanks, aerial torpedoes and flame-throwing tanks.

My people at the Company Club are roasting and cooking away. We're eating plum compote and apple fritters. They taste wonderful. I'm getting a terrific rest now. Really. I'm relaxed and not at all nervous. It's very good for me to be with the Company again.

Friday, 19th September 1941

It was bitter cold in the night; you can't sleep in the open any more. It rains now and then too, which makes things worse.

In the morning I accompany the C.O. into the town [Piryatin]; although it is forbidden to enter and this order is being checked by the M.P.s, we manage to get in. I can't describe how the enemy vehicles in the town look, and how many there are—at least 2,000. In a curve they were standing four abreast, apparently knocked out by our Stukas. Hundreds of skeleton vehicles were sitting there, burned out right down to the iron frame.

I grab one of the intact cars and intend to drive it to our Company. The M.P. won't let me out of the town with it, though, so I sneak out with the car, using devious streets. Finally we're allowed to enter town and find quarters there. We had enough of the cold last night, too. There is just time to wash and shave before it gets dark. The kitchen wants to make Wiener Schnitzel tomorrow if we stay here till noon. I shall certainly accept that! The whole detail is in the sack by 7.30—we might have to get up at the crack of dawn, after all.

Saturday, 20th September 1941

In the early morning we march off back through Lubny in the direction of Tischky again. It's beautiful, like the loveliest summer day. As far as I could learn, we're to do a mopping-up job between the three rivers Uday, Sulliza and Sula.

A Russian regiment is supposed to be fleeing towards the south. According to the prisoners we've taken, several groups of staff officers are in this three-rivers region—they are supposed to have got away from the battle of Kiev. That lures us on, of course. The C.O. and our Battalion decide to chase the enemy regiments at once.

After passing through the first village, we spread out over the fields. Beforehand we are assigned some tanks, and now we've spread out the tanks and other vehicles in a broad formation over the fields and are charging into the fleeing Russians. The order of the Companies and other units has got a bit mixed up in the intoxication of this fabulous chase, but it's wonderful to watch the vehicles tearing ahead. There ought to be some newsreel men here; there would be incomparable picture material! Tanks and armoured cars, the men sitting on them, encrusted with a thick coating of dirt, heady with the excitement of the attack—haystacks set on fire by our tank cannons, running Russians, hiding, surrendering! It's a marvellous sight!

We take a few prisoners: most of them have to be dragged out from under haystacks or flushed out of the furrows. Shy, unbelieving, filled with terror, they come. Many a Bolshevik has to lay down his life here—his stupid pigheadedness and his fear (drilled into him) have to be paid for by his death.

Monday, 22nd September 1941

In the morning the C.O. let me know that I shall probably be ordered to the Battalion—as battle clerk. I immediately rushed there to try to kill this idea, but all my excuses don't do me any good. Until further notice I am to be attached to Battalion. And I have no desire to go there at all.

Wednesday, 24th September 1941

At 04.00 I had a motor-cycle from Company come and fetch me. It's overcast and rather cool today. In Romny we stop for a bit, and there I learn that we are to relieve the 3rd or 4th Armoured Division.

Before darkness we arrive in Galatschinjar, just in time to set up quarters: there aren't very many possibilities anyway, just a few filthy, lousy huts—that's all. If you could experience just one of the nights of which we spend so many, Henny, you simply wouldn't believe that people could stand it. Yes, and that people never know anything else their whole lives. But these Russians can't be people any more, they must be immune to any sort of feelings now; otherwise it wouldn't be possible for 180,000,000 people to put up with it.

Friday, 26th September 1941

Because of the rain the past days, the roads and paths are completely soft, so that the vehicles often slide into the ditch.

I've had such frightful toothache since yesterday that I could bang my head against the wall. No powder helps, either. It would be the best thing to have it pulled. I twist in my bed from one side to the other.

You should see the act the civilians put on when we make it clear to them that we intend to use their sties to sleep in. A weeping and yelling begin, as if their throats were being cut, until we chuck them out. Whether young or old, man or wife, they stand in their rags and tatters on the doorstep and can't be persuaded to go to their neighbours or to the empty houses. When we finally threaten them at pistol point, they disappear for a few minutes, only to return again yelling even more loudly.

Sunday, 28th September 1941

We move ahead very slowly. It begins to rain several times. There's a wind as bad as the worst autumn days. It's not the first time that we sleep in the vehicles, but it's very unpleasant now. Terribly cold. You can't wrap yourself in too many blankets. When I think back on the July and August days, when we simply spent the nights lying in a field on the grass, I have to mourn for the summer, which is ending now. And who knows what's in front of us as far as the weather goes?

I've put on my boots and wrapped my feet in blankets: and this way the night is not so bad. The wind whistles through the canvas of the lorries as if it were a birdcage and blows the rain in. It's freezing cold. In spite of this, we listen to our beloved 'Lili Marlene' at 22.00 hours on our army wireless set.

Monday, 29th September 1941

In the early morning we make a camp fire out of the hay-stacks, but it only warms the side you turn towards the fire, while the other goes on freezing. The summer really is finished. The rain is depressingly regular. The roads, which are mud anyway, will be quite impassable. And what these mean for an armoured division, anyone can see. If we all had tank tracks, or at least four-wheel drive, we could make the grade. But the way it is, the wheels just spin in the deep mud and you can't even get the vehicles started.

Tuesday, 30th September 1941

In spite of the continual rain, most of our vehicles caught up with us during the night. It's a miracle! I had only just started a letter to you when we got orders from Regiment to begin the retreat to Konnlitschka. You can't start anything!

The chief and I drive ahead to find a faintly passable road. There isn't such a thing. The best thing to do is to go across fields. And that means keeping on the look-out against losing your way. The kitchen can only be moved ahead with the whole Company helping to push them along.

Thursday, 2nd October 1941

It's the same all over Russia: a monotonous, endless plain, here and there broken by hollows or valleys in which there is generally a brook or a stream. In these hollows there are little villages made out of clay and excreta, or at best out of wood with a straw roof.

Time has stood still in this country for at least 500 years. Clay and wood and straw existed then, also horses and cows and tallow too, which is what they still use for fuel. And shit has been around as long as people have. Really—that's the way it is here. Perhaps the few large industrial towns are an exception, but they're only a façade anyway.

At 18.00 we arrive in Tschernatscha and after a lot of discussion we finally find quarters in one of their impossible pig sties. The owner runs his legs off for us. Water to wash in appears at once: we're quite unrecognizable in our crust of dirt. So I give him a few cigarettes. Do you suppose he ever smoked anything that good in his life before?

Friday, 3rd October 1941

You notice clearly now that autumn has made its appearance punctually. And then the question arises: which is better, to be moving and to sweat more *with* a coat and then to shiver less when you're quiet, or to go on as we've been doing, without one? The C.O. says we can't move as well in a coat. Is he right? Well, his is the bigger pay-packet, and so it's no coats for us!

When we set up quarters for the night, we set up our wireless set as usual, which only takes a few minutes; and we nearly fall flat on our faces when we realize that the Führer is about to speak. I've been a soldier now for quite a while—a battle soldier, too. And I really know what our men prefer, if they could choose between mail from home—letters and parcels—or a quiet, undisturbed night, or listening to one of the Führer's speeches.

No one knows what this beloved voice means to us—how our cheeks glow, our eyes sparkle, when the Führer takes the war criminals to task. What a lift his words give us, as we crowd round the wireless set, not wanting to miss a single word! Is there a finer reward after a day of battle than to hear the Führer? Never! We all of us thank him!

Saturday, 4th October 1941

The quiet selfless courage of a dispatch rider, who dashes about in the midst of the bullets, right through murderous mortar fire, despite the worst enemy artillery fire, cannot be praised highly enough. Or the medical orderly, who can only crawl along to a wounded man and then crawl back again, and just as he is about to jump back into our emplacement is himself wounded, but takes care of three other wounded men before he says: 'Now it's my turn,' lets down his trousers, and binds up a bullet wound, 15 inches long and grazing very deep. What is there to say? Can anyone understand, can anyone imagine what Germany's finest men have done in this war?

Monday, 6th October 1941

At 08.30 we march off, as last Company. It rained in torrents the whole night. As usual, there's no road to speak about; it's nothing but a path across the fields. Today it's possibly even worse than the way back to Konnlitschka. The fields are completely soft, and only here and there one of the signs our troops stuck into the ground shows us the way. If we couldn't see the tracks we would be bound to get lost.

At night it gets really cold now, and we all think that it can't go on much longer. In this morass we shall soon be unable to move at all. Our baggage train couldn't even make the grade today. What will it be like in the rainy period?

Tuesday, 7th October 1941

Tonight we had the first real Russian snowstorm. The snow didn't stay on the ground, but the wind whistled through every nook and cranny of our hut, and we expected the straw roof to take off at any moment. A nice foretaste of the coming winter. That can be a real mess! (Personally I think we'll have to be pulled out of action this month.) We've not much more petrol, and none will come for quite a while because our tankers are standing way back and it'll take them a long time to get through all the mud.

Tomorrow we're to storm the town of Dmitriyev, 5 km. in front of us. Everyone is saying that this is to be our last job, and that the Division will rendezvous in D. It would be the best thing, too, for all the Companies are thoroughly beaten up, and many of the vehicles are already knocked out. If it really does go on, though, it would be better to create a battalicn out of the regiment; then it could be properly equipped with men and machines and would be ready for battle.

The rain still hasn't let up. It's worth watching our battle vehicles work through the mud. The Steyr[1] really is indestructible.

Wednesday, 8th October 1941

Some enemy positions are still blocking the eastern entry to D[mitriyev], but using hand grenades and pistols we get the Russians out of their caves and fox-holes. They must be thoroughly impressed by our fire; their eyes are filled with fear, and they certainly can't understand why we aren't mowing them down right away. 'Stalin kaputt': with these words they are taken off to the prison camps. It's a better life for them than under the whips of the commissars. For them, the war's finished.

While combing the town, we receive a few shots from concealed Russians, but otherwise it's entirely empty. It's not until we rush across to the bridges at the other end of town, which we want to secure, that the civilians show themselves. The C.O. and I run with an MG unit as fast as our legs can carry us, but just as we round the last corner, the bridge blows sky-high with a deafening explosion. A Russian can still be seen, running across the other one; we shoot at him, but too late. Apparently he prepared the explosives and lit the fuse, because right afterwards the second bridge blows up, too.

A wrecked Russian armoured scouting car is sitting on the street, and as we look inside it, a Russian climbs out. He was the driver, and was anxiously awaiting our arrival though he was afraid we'd shoot him. But his common sense won. Someone explains to him in Russian that nothing will happen to him,

[1] The Steyr, originally a factory for civilian motor-cars and trucks, had its headquarters in the Upper Austrian town of Steyr.

whereupon he wants to embrace all of us, and is quite willing to give us information about everything.

When we've established our security units, we go and look for a house near the bridge. The one we picked is the best I've ever seen in Russia. With real furniture, proper rooms—a real treat for us. The people there were very afraid at the beginning, they were especially terrified that we would shoot their 17-year-old son. But when we've assured them nothing will happen, they become friendly and bring us milk, butter, honey, warm some water for us and serve us hand and foot. Is it respect on their part, or is it fear of the German soldier?

When I have to go to Battalion in the afternoon, I have a good look at D. As usual, a hideous place. The only decent building is a barracks, and the 8·8 flak is already ensconced there for our air raid protection. Apart from that the customary miserable, small, filthy huts. In the evening we learn that we are to stay here for the present—one or two days of quiet—marvellous!

Friday, 10th October 1941

We haven't seen any pay in God knows how long, but that doesn't really matter, because in this promised land there's nothing to buy anyway and now we've each of us several hundred marks in the pocket.

The unpleasant part of this fast advance is that the supply trains can't catch up to us through the mud. We haven't had any mail for an eternity, and what's worse, we can't mail any letters ourselves. For although nothing can happen to you at home—and everything goes on there as usual—still, you will be worrying about us, and that's very unfortunate.

Monday, 13th October 1941

Snow and rain alternate the whole time, and the ground flatly refuses to harden up. It only freezes at night, when it's cold, but at 07.00 in the morning it thaws again. There is no more petrol at all. Now and then we get a can or two in D[mitriyev]. We here can't understand how it gets here at all, if you think of the roads and the weather.

No trace of the mess convoy either. We bake our bread in D. using captured flour stores. Now we are getting to know the second, unpleasant side of the war. But that can't upset us, naturally. So long as chickens and geese are to be found, and potatoes, it's all right. That's our daily food now. There are also enough pigs running about, and what with a few eggs and some milk, we do well enough.

The baggage train is reported to have been set on and captured by the Russians. We're very put out about that, but especially me, because my trunk was in the baggage train. If the Russians broke into it and threw my printed notepaper, my books and my diaries all over the street—that must be a funny sight. What happened to our major at Shdany[1] will probably happen to me, too: that's my punishment for my having amused myself at his expense then.

The way the Russians look, their life, their flats and a lot of other things, I shall describe later. We call the civilians flea machines. That'll do for the present.

We hardly know when it's Sunday in this war. Every day is the same, and we have none of civilization's benefits; if we didn't have our marvellous army radio transmitter, we'd be really at sixes and sevens. But at least we can hear the news, music, lectures, and at the end of each day Lili Marlene.

Tuesday, 14th October 1941

Today we received orders that we are to be attached to the 1st Battalion, and are to march to Fatezh tonight. There's no point in trying to move during the day; the mud would not allow it. We can make it only during the night, when the earth is frozen hard.

There's still no trace of our baggage train. Our M./S. Spiess

[1] Major Gutmann's car had been attacked by the Russians; the Major and his driver escaped, but the Russians spread the car's contents all over the ground in wild and slightly amusing disorder.

has gone back to see if he can't at least bring the mess car up front.

Wednesday, 15th October 1941

At 11.15 we reach Linez. Many vehicles are still missing, left behind stuck fast in the mud. It's really a piece of luck to get through at all.

What should I say of the village? The dullness, the hopeless grey of Russia, the poverty of the people, the messy, dirty and lousy appearance of all the huts—all this seldom changes. Nothing, but nothing, to lighten the eye. If I only think of a single flower garden in Holland, the neat streets along the pretty little houses, the people—it's the difference between heaven and hell. One just can't describe it, one has to see it to believe it.

Monday, 20th October 1941

Who brings the rumours, and who thinks them up, you never know. All at once everyone's saying: winter quarters in Russia. If it weren't so ridiculous, one might believe it. But here's the situation: we as an armoured division, which is used to driving into the enemy and pushing him in front of us, whose name is only mentioned by the Russians as 'the terror of the Ukraine' or 'the yellow SS', we with our vehicles are supposed to spend the icy winter in Russia, especially when we've been way up front since the very beginning; we whose successes have been so numerous, *we* are supposed to spend the winter in Russia. Impossible! is all I have to say to that.

Unfortunately three things happened in the Companies that can only be thoroughly condemned. One lieutenant, a platoon leader, apparently lost his nerve during a Russian attack and fled with his men, without informing his neighbours. Incidentally, there weren't any Russians at all where the platoon was stationed and they never showed up afterwards either. Rather comic.

Two noncoms are known to have shot themselves in the hand.

Out of fear for their personal safety and hoping in this way to be able to lead a quieter and less dangerous life. They are the only three such occurrences in this war I know of; but regrettably, they did happen. It's scandalous, not only for themselves, but for the companies. What do they think? What makes them different from the Russians? I shall never understand it. Let's hope they get punished properly.

Tuesday, 21st October 1941

A scouting party which went to Radobesh yesterday reports that the place is without any enemy troops. Immediately we send out a unit to requisition food. Goose every day is dull and unhealthy besides. The whole Company heart, as it were, laughed when Mayer, Pichler and the interpreter reappeared with butter, eggs, cream, potatoes, honey and a pig. Terrific all these treats! The pig is slaughtered at once, and a few minutes later our hut is smelling of the roast.

Today I wrote numerous postcards and letters. If they only get as far as D[mitriyev], that's a big step forward, for there's an army post office already installed there. It doesn't matter so much if we don't get mail; we don't have to worry about you at home; but you worry about us, and that gives rise to the curious situation: it is better to give news than to receive.

Friday, 24th October 1941

On the whole it's quiet now; the Russians in our immediate neighbourhood are gone. The rain stops only for a few hours at a time. Everything is grey, dark and impenetrable. The whole of Russia is sunk in mud.

Saturday, 25th October 1941

At 09.30 we push off towards Shdanovo, which is only a few km. away; but the mud is now knee-high and won't allow us to get to S. before evening. Even getting out of Linez is a real problem for our routine drivers, but what goes on along the march route defies description. Many vehicles get stuck after the first few metres and can only be freed with the combined assistance of everyone present.

Our drivers have now had experience in four campaigns. They mastered the ploughed fields of Poland, the swift tempo in Holland, the breathless chase in France, the mountains of the Balkans; they drive in pitch darkness, without lights, as safely as if it were bright sunshine. But the worst of the lot is undoubtedly the Soviet Union; and yet they master that, too—many of them with the last drop of petrol. They are worthy to stand side by side with the brave fighters in battle.

At 14.00 the first vehicles arrive in S.

Monday, 27th October 1941

Today, here in Fatezh, there is petrol, and food too. How *did* they get it here? It's all a mystery. Mail leaves, too, perhaps via the main road between Kursk and Orel.

In the evening there's a C.O.'s conference again, which turns out to have tremendous consequences for us; something we never dreamed of—our Companies, with reinforcements, are to undertake a large-scale reconnaissance action towards Kursk. No one wants to believe it, because we never expected such a thing; we're all terribly depressed. But as is so often the case, that can't really shake us. On the contrary, after being 'down' for a few minutes—because we can't have all our wishes come true—our thoughts all turn to Kursk, and we're full of, and delighted with, our new job. That's the wonderful thing about this war, how quickly you change your attitude.

Tuesday, 28th October 1941

Thinking about today, which will probably be a tough one, and worrying about waking up in time, I had a very bad night. I got up at 3.30, and packed and loaded by the light of a candle.

We go to the collecting point in driving snow-*cum*-rain: our rendezvous is on the main road to Kursk. It's still pitch-black, and the town is completely still. It sounds ghostly as the people move forward, the weapons clatter, and the few vehicles roll along.

At 6.30 Major Gutmann, who is running the whole show, comes along. The task of Operation Gutmann is to advance along the road towards Kursk, find out the condition of the road, the bridges, the surrounding countryside, and if possible to discover which enemy units are in Kursk. A nice task for us: with a bit of luck we could crown this enterprise with the capture of K. That would be terrific!

The road is good: incredible as it sounds, it's a real concrete road! Yes, something like this *does* exist in Russia. So you see, this paradise isn't nearly so bad as they say (?!). Ah, it's that naughty Nazi propaganda again!

There are *in toto* three bridges between here and Kursk; they are sure to be destroyed, all of them. That doesn't bother the C.O., however; he looks for a detour. And finds one. First we have to blow up some mines which the Russians set up for us near the new bridge. Unfortunately, this bridge is so unsteady and weak that the two tanks cannot possibly cross it. They can't go through the water either, because the riverbed is too deep and has too soft a bottom. We have to leave the tanks behind.

Nevertheless, on we go. After the detour, some of our vehicles get stuck and have to be pulled out by the flak and PAK. Once again we hit the road and make fine time. We never had anything so good in Russia before. Not a Russian is to be seen—not even in the woods which appear now and then. No movements at all. We get to the second bridge, which is of course blown up. A detour seems at first sight impossible, and all our searching is of no use. All our bright ideas to improvise something are no good, either. Here was where Operation Gutmann came to an end. Unfortunately.

We spend the night—naturally, the 6th Company bears the brunt—in a place behind the second, destroyed bridge. Tomorrow the whole Battalion is to follow along.

Wednesday, 29th October 1941

The night was simply freezing. And we froze particularly, since we had neither blankets or overcoats. The rain has stopped, and the streets and fields are frozen solid.

In the afternoon we hear the first news about our baggage train. When we were going through Romny, we took in some replacements; however they stayed with the baggage and went along with it the whole time. One of these men has now made his way to us and related what happened. Because of the frightful road conditions, the supply column couldn't follow us after Amon. It crawled along, a metre at a time, to the next village. Some of the vehicles will have managed by now to get as far as Dmitriyev (my God!).

The village in which the main body was staying was attacked by the Russians. The vehicles had to be abandoned and the personnel ran away. Their flight was a mad adventure; the enemy was constantly shooting at them, and in the broad swamps we may possibly have lost some men.

I got paler and paler as I heard this tale, and all my thoughts were of my trunk, my lost shirts and so on, my books, my work, letters. I could have fallen on the man's neck when I heard that the lorry in which my trunk and the C.O.'s were stowed, was not attacked in the village and robbed, but had gone on and must have reached Dmitriyev by now. I breathed a sigh of relief.

Saturday, 1st November 1941

In the few hours of sleep we could snatch, the orders to attack Kursk came through. At last a real city. We expect a lot from it; after all, it's—after Kiev—the oldest city in Russia. The heights south of Kassinovo are full of enemy. The Russians spent the night together with us in Kassinovo. We didn't know of their existence, nor did they of ours. It could be out of a film!

You can see clearly the Russian defences—trenches, and so forth. And a few moments later, our blessings flow over them in the form of all our MGs, heavy mortars and artillery, pounding the position and mashing up its defenders. And keeping them down flat. Under cover of all these heavy weapons, our men from the Company move forward towards the Russians a jump at a time; and in one swoop they are on them, yelling 'Hurrah'. Those who don't surrender after a short round from the machine pistol are mowed down by an MG. It's a bloody business.

The Russians now see the danger threatening them on their left flank, and they seek their safety in flight; but they forgot one little thing, namely that the Germanskis can run too, to wit after the enemy. Few of us remember that they are armed, for we're all filled with the thought of capturing the Bolsheviks. A fabulous race begins, the Russians tearing off, a part of our Company hot in pursuit, that old daredevil, the indestructible Karkosch out in front. It's not easy to catch up with the Russians, for they have the edge on us. When they see that we're catching up on them all the same, they throw away the few weapons they took with them in an attempt to escape capture. But our boys come nearer and nearer—so close that they stretch out their hands to grab the Russians by the neck and throw them down. It's a wonderful, incredibly funny sight. Unforgettable! That would have been something for the newsreel boys!

At 12.00 the attack on Kursk begins. The major, energetic as ever and (as in every battle) up in front, with an encouraging word for every one of us, says: 'Squeeze that tube, boys, there are quarters waiting for us in Kursk.' And brother, do we squeeze that tube! We all want to get to a real bed.

In quick march, preceded by the tanks, we move up far enough to have the city lying in front of us. To the left we see some enemy positions which probably won't be dangerous for us, but the tanks fire at them anyway. The Russians leave their trenches and run like rabbits. We avoid a minefield, marking it as we go past, and then we're in front of the north-east side of Kursk. All over the place you can see trenches, MG installations and fox-holes, but the Russians have preferred to disappear. Better for them, better for us.

Is it the wish to be the first man in Kursk? Or is it the hope of a bed? Or is it that we want to get out of the enemy artillery line of fire? Anyway, running like a bunch of pigs, we reach the first houses of Kursk. Night is already upon us. We find ourselves in a street in a suburb of Kursk—lots of small, hideous huts.

To look for a decent house is pointless. There aren't any. Moreover, our artillery has broken every pane of glass in town. Now we can curse them—there's not a room in town without draughts! Despite it all, we lie down and sleep the sleep of the just.

Saturday, 2nd November 1941

At 09.00 we start to take over the city. Civilians inform us that the streets are full of barricades and that a lot of mines have been laid to hinder our progress. The Red Army has cleared out, but armed a lot of partisans beforehand. This can be tricky.

Of the 120,000 inhabitants, 30,000 are said to have fled to Voronezh. Like yesterday, many buildings were burning during the night. Blown-up bridges and railway installations bear witness to the destructive fury of the Soviets.

The first minutes go fine. Distrustful, we look into all the side streets, into all the windows—partisans can be hidden anywhere, and they want to slit our throats. In front of a church the C.O. orders a halt. With a connoisseur's glance, he takes in the curious mixture of clay and wooden huts and houses, and after curt orders to the Platoons, we move on swiftly. And not a bit too soon. A few minutes later, as the regimental battle headquarters reached the church, the partisans' bullets were whistling round the tower. And from this moment, our unopposed advance is at an end. Every second a bullet wings past us. You never know where it comes from. Pressed flat against the house walls, bent down, your gun ready to shoot, your grenade in the other hand, you creep along.

Several times we shoot at suspicious-looking places, straight from the hip with our MG; all round you can hear the dull thuds of hand grenades exploding.

Some civilians, who despite our order don't stand still, are shot down. We get to a street crossing, which some partisans are raking with excellently placed and well aimed fire. Some of our men get across; the fifth meets up with a bullet and rolls down a short incline. To go on across this square would only mean unnecessary losses, and some of our men have grasped the situation at once and turn left, without waiting for any orders.

Then we get to the first barricades. The MGs set up and rake them, and the Platoons go ahead.

'Watch out for mines,' yells the C.O., and not a second too soon: the first men were about to trot right over a mine. Left and right of the barricade they left a small passage open which was strewn with mines. One hundred metres farther on we hit a main street. Shots come from all over. Some civilians whisk into a house and at that moment we have another wounded man on our hands. Armed civilians and suspicious characters on the one hand, wounded on the other—who can wonder if we mow down everything in our path. It was quite a difficult job to do this in the case of two drunk Russians we met.

We stay at this main crossing a long while, until the white Verey lights of the Battalion and infantry show us that they've reached the same depth of penetration farther along the line; then we push on. A few hundred metres away there's another barricade. We can clearly spot some civilians as they take up their places behind the installation. MGs shoot at it, and the heavy mortars fire a few well-placed shots into the barricade. It's not long before some of the accursed partisans turn tail and run. After knocking off a few more civilians, we get almost as far as the city limits. A river blocks our advance, but there are only a few huts on the other side anyway. Our target is reached, and we are now to return to the main crossing for rendezvous.

Kursk is in our hands. A new special news announcement will be winging through the ether. And our Division did it. Meanwhile the city has calmed down. More and more of our soldiers move in, and thus the weak partisan opposition becomes useless.

Civilians come out of their houses, look at us, and can't get over it that we don't touch anyone who is unarmed. At last they even invite us into their homes and offer us tea. In front of a burning house, we manage to save several crates of complete intact tobacco. A tracer-shell from one of our MGs set one of the finest houses in K. on fire: irony of fate!

We do find quite a nice place, though—real furniture, large windows, and best of all a bed.

Monday, 11th November 1941

Unfortunately we still have to put up with some partisan stupidities—one dead, one wounded in our ranks. Although a house round the corner from us was mined, and it was forbidden to go into it, two of our people couldn't resist searching it. They climbed in through a window and got into one of the rooms through an open door. In there was a desk—the place had been the 'House of the Red Army'—and one of the drawers was half open, so that you could see a little pistol inside. One of them opened the drawer, and the next moment there was a frightful explosion. A leg and an arm torn off, the other with light wounds: he could drag himself out. We couldn't save the one who was badly wounded, for in five minutes the house was in flames from attic to cellar. He burned in there.

The Engineers are busily clearing the whole city of mines, but of course they can't be everywhere at the same time.

Tuesday, 18th November 1941

At 14.00 our C.O. was ordered to report to the regimental aide-de-camp. I thought he was going to get the German Cross in gold, or was ordered there for some other reason. I thought of innumerable possibilities, but neither I nor anyone else guessed the right one. We almost fell over. We innocent angels thought we had in front of us some pleasant weeks which we would spend next to nice warm stoves; we hadn't a clue what our superiors had in store for us. All those dire prophesies had something to them. Now they've caught up with us: we are to advance in the direction of Voronezh! But now comes the most interesting part: we are to go *on foot*! We've become infantry! How fatuous!

I don't get angry, though. An old soldier's proverb says: 'Don't be angry; just marvel.' And all you can do the whole time you serve is to marvel. So I laughed, and laughed heartily, out of malicious joy at my own misfortune.

Sunday, 30th November 1941

You couldn't expect anything different. We, the tail end of the Division, caught up with everyone—all our motorized units—on foot, walked 35 km., in the past few days, arrived at the very front of the Division, had to take over security duty in the night and now we're to advance 12 km., on foot, and then attack. Right in the front line. It had to happen. Moreover today is Sunday. Well, we'll survive.

At 09.00 we fall in. Some of our men have white cloths round the upper parts of their bodies and over their helmets as a camouflage against the snow. We plod off. The weather is good to us—a weak wind. So we're doing all right. At 12.00 we approach today's goal. There's not a sound out of the place, so it's presumably free of the enemy. As we get to the first houses, a noncom from the 2nd Platoon steps on a mine; it blows off his feet up to the knees and also his right thumb. He looks horrible. Probably he can't be saved either.

We find the billets assigned to us and set up security units on the east, though it's very unlikely we shall be attacked.

Monday, 1st December 1941

At 07.00 we're off. It's snowing hard and a strong wind is up. Terrible weather for marching: many in the Companies have foot trouble already. We've got a lot of characters with flat feet, fallen arches, etc.—not at all suitable as foot soldiers.

We're supposed to find shelter in a village some 6 km. to the north, but when we get there, we find the entire village consists of exactly 2 huts—scarcely room for a single group. So we have to go on, another 8 km. or so. The other Companies roll past us, often with a sarcastic smile for us poor limping chaps. We slowly limp into the next place, where we are assigned 3 small huts and 3 so-called Russian houses—one room for a platoon of 39 men. They can barely stand up inside, and that's where they are supposed to spend the night. I can't stand that idea, so I go and fetch the aide-de-camp so he can see our plight for himself. This isn't a war any more but a fight for billets. And we've done 100 km. now, and no end in sight.

Tuesday, 2nd December 1941

It was an awful night. At 08.00 we're on our way again; again we have about 15 km. in front of us. It's snowing again, with a sharp wind, and freezing cold. The beards which we've let grow from the time we left Kursk have icicles hanging off them. We learn that we are to stay in this region and make our winter quarters here. It's a situation too disgusting to contemplate. Ah, the Russian campaign! We're starting the sixth month now.

Sunday, 7th December 1941

Yesterday we had 32 degrees below zero [centigrade]. It will get worse. We are not advancing any more, however. All that can happen is that we are moved within this neighbourhood. The villages lying in front of us are burned down now, so that the Russians can't use them against us. Behind us on the hills bunkers will be constructed as a winter defence line. Probably we shall move back from here, too, and burn down all these villages behind us. The border for the winter is thus the Tim Valley.

The population really isn't to be envied. But all softer emotions must be sacrificed for tactical necessity. Supposedly the Russians are also pursuing the same course on their side.

I only don't understand what is to happen to us. Are we, an armoured division, supposed to sit in a bunker? We've got to freshen up; is this to happen in Kursk? Or in Poland? Or in Germany? Or even in Vienna? There is one rumour after another on this subject. And I, with my inborn optimism, still believe that we shall get to Germany sometime. We've certainly earned it.

Friday, 12th December 1941

Yesterday we learned that the names of two worthy and deserving men in each company are to be turned in by tomorrow for home leave. I'm one of the two. Hurrah! To be at home on Christmas Eve? That would be the loveliest Christmas present.

I feel a bit like a coward, a deserter, who leaves his Kameraden sitting out on the limb. Moreover, I never thought of going before Christmas, but now that the possibility exists, I can barely wait. Private First-class Möslinger was to have gone with me. Father of 6 children. This afternoon he fell, a splinter from a Russian shell got him. Isn't that tragic?

Saturday, 13th December 1941

Today I learned more about my leave: on the 17th I have to be in Orel. To be de-loused! On the 18th the train leaves, and gets to Vienna in 4½ days. Marvellous! Just in time for Christmas. My God! I'm looking forward to it so! I intend to leave at seven tomorrow with my companion and our three students who are getting leave.[1]

Sunday, 14th December 1941[2]

At 05.00 we received a wireless message: 'Leaves postponed. Order follows.' Typical brass again! We only heard by accident that there would be leave for two men at all, and we heard about it some days later; but when it's cancelled, they get the message to us in a few hours. If I had only left right away yesterday evening!

[1] Students were occasionally allowed to continue their studies after having served a certain length of time.

[2] This part of the diary, from 14th–23rd December incl., was added later, on Christmas Eve. We have placed it here in its proper chronological position.

17TH DECEMBER 1941

Wednesday, 17th December 1941

At 04.00 alarm is sounded. Supported by artillery, the Russians attack to the north of the railway. I and my Platoon are reserve; I collect them and wait for orders at a particularly vulnerable point. Just as I am at Company battle headquarters to put myself in the picture, we notice that the Russians are coming straight at us. To the right of a ruin which lies in front of us, I can see them jumping about. Gradually the fire power of the Platoon that the 2nd Company installed here has become weakened; almost all the MGs have been knocked out!

Without waiting for orders, I place the Platoon between the houses and spread out the carbines. Meanwhile the enemy artillery has stopped, for the Russians are already quite near us. It's still pitch dark, and there isn't any point in firing yet since you can't see your targets clearly. After a moment's thought, I've worked out my plan: one MG is to shoot continually at the Russians lying in front of us, using short bursts, so as to keep them from advancing. The other MGs and all those with carbines are to go into position, I shall have a white Verey light shot up, and in that moment we shall aim and shoot with all our various weapons.

I stand up in front of a house so as to see everything; then I give the order: 'Ready! When you see the Verey light go up, shoot as fast as you can, keep it low off the ground. Aim, boys! White Verey lights, FIRE!'

For 9 seconds it's like broad daylight, you can see the whole ground in front of us. The Russians have advanced to within 100 metres. But my boys are already shooting like mad so as to use every bit of the light. Then it's dark again. With a few machine-gun bursts I keep the Russians down, then I yell again.

Three Russians, using a row of trees as protection, got as far as the houses: we finish them off with hand grenades. In the light of the many Verey lights, you can see clearly that some of the Russians have already disappeared towards the rear; but there are plenty of them left in front of us. We're all praying for it to get light: the Verey lights are getting short.

As the first faint light appears, I send an MG forward to the ruin, so as to work on the Bolshevik's flank. Slowly it gets light, and now the enemy is lying in front of us on a silver plate. The minute we see any of them trying to get away, they've already had it.

Another thing is revealed by the light, too: without a bit of cover the Platoon was lying and standing in front of, and between, the houses. Nothing could persuade them to seek cover at the expense of good visibility. Many of them stood straight up to fire with their carbines, though the bullets were whining all round them. One of them stood in a window to shoot, one of them was posted on the roof with a telescope range on his gun, one of them knelt in front of a chair which he used to support his carbine, the MG boys established themselves at the corners of the houses and huts—all shooting and shooting with but one thought: the Russians must not break through, otherwise it's the end. Truly, the boys really acted courageously.

At 08.00 I remember a system which has proved so satisfactory in the past. I order a cease-fire, and when there isn't a gun working on our side, I yell at the top of my lungs to the Russians: 'Rucki wjerch! . . .'—'Hands up! Surrender!' One by one, the hands go up. When a whole group in a bush appears, I go towards the Russians with my carbine men, however not without telling the MGs to watch carefully and to fire at once if any one of the other side shoots. You can never tell with those rats!

The prisoners are herded together into a house, but there aren't as many as we'd expected. When we return, we discover the reason: the many dead that are still there. All shot through the head. My men shot well, you've got to hand it to them. Some of the dead are still burning, set on fire by our Verey lights. Then we start counting: 50 prisoners and 150 dead just in my Platoon's area. A tremendous success!

In the afternoon, an enemy railway tank column rolls up to within 4 km. of the town, stays there, and shoots at us half an hour before it turns round and whisks off. You could see it easily from the 1st Platoon's position. I simply don't understand that our planes don't do something. The Russians are bringing up reserves all the time; they unload them right in front of our noses, their pioneers repair the destroyed bridges along the railway line, they attack us in droves—and probably not only in this region; and we can't do anything against them. If it goes on like this, they'll crush us with their numerical superiority alone.

Friday, 19th December 1941

Our people are kaputt. You've got to say it; and see why: one hour outside, one hour in the hut, watch, alarm sentry duty, listening duty, observer duty, occupy the MG posts—one thing after another. It wouldn't surprise me to see some of them break down. This has been going on since 28th November, since our departure from Besedino. When you figure: for weeks and weeks one hour of sleep, then one hour on duty, what that means!

Sunday, 21st December 1941

At 04.00 I brought the few vehicles left into Krasnaya-Polyana. I couldn't really say how I got there, because I could just as well have landed in the Russians' laps—which almost happened to an artillery column that wanted to retreat, and which I could just manage to stop as they were proceeding towards Marmyzhi railway station.

It has been snowing for days now, and you can't recognize the road at all. Moreover there was such a fog last night that you couldn't see 5 metres in front of you. A Verey light would have had no effect, because they give out only a weak, milky white light.

I drove very slowly, feeling my way along. I didn't even see the woods that were mined, didn't see Rasschojwez either. I just tried to reach the railway so that I could turn sharp left—to the west—and as I crossed the Tim, I knew it was all right. When I counted the vehicles, I saw we had 5. Out of 40!

Exhausted and beaten, we looked for a house where we could

stay. We found two little huts for the Platoon; in ours an old, almost starving man was dying. I left the vehicles on the road with a sign on them so that the others would know. In the morning one after another comes along, till at noon they are all there.

Monday, 22nd December 1941

Shall I tell you how we waited for day to come? So that we could at last escape this dungeon, and go and find houses where we would have enough room, where we could heat the place and warm ourselves up. We cursed this war—yes, *this* war—with every curse that our fertile soldier brains could invent. And in all this cursing and swearing, in all this cold, in all this Kameradschaft (which a night like this offers), a new and glorious page was written in the great song of the German soldier.[1] It was only for a moment, only a gesture, during which this indestructible German soldiery again showed itself—only the fraction of a second in which one saw that with these men we cannot be vanquished.

A word cut outside through the dawn, echoing in the cold of this December night, shook them awake, these marvellous soldiers, from the positions where they had dropped like sacks the night before; and despite the previous cursing and swearing, despite the exhaustion, despite everything (they had really fought like lions)——

'Alarm!'

That was enough! As if stung by a tarantula, one grabbed his gun, another his ammunition, a third his gear, and exploded out of the house to stop the enemy in his advance. Eight hundred metres away they are moving towards us.

Verey lights explode, lighting up the whole landscape, and by their light our men took up their positions (which had been pointed out to them earlier); but as if everyone suspected what was happening, not a single shot was fired. Ever more clearly the words started to reach us:

[1] This and other mixed metaphors are of Prüller's invention.

'Don't shoot; it's us.'

It was the 8th Company which was coming back in the face of regiments of Russians advancing from Tjoploje who threatened to crush them. The whole horizon is now black with Russians, they tell us, and wave after wave follows one another.

The situation is slowly getting serious, and some people are getting nervous. And so we get orders to fill our positions to the last man. Just as the 2nd Platoon is distributing rations, a tank shell rips into the house, another shell hits nearby. Result: 19 knocked out, 6 of them are dead. Awful. I take the 2nd Platoon, now almost non-existent, into position, and then go round to the 3rd. I don't see anything of the Russians yet, but behind some trees I think I see a well-camouflaged Russian tank. When I look through my glass, I see I'm right.

At once I have the 3·7 cm. PAK, who are in position nearby, informed, and they change their place at once. But at the same instant the tank starts to tear in our direction, across the street, through the hollow, and right up to our front lines, past them and on. PAK shoots at it, the shells ricochet off! It's one of the dreaded Christie tanks. Our C.O. is running for his life, a few feet in front of the tank, falls, the tank shoots at him, misses, crashes past him. Then the tank turns to the left and starts to play hide and seek round the house corners with our men.

I watch all this with horror. But worse is to come, for in all this excitement another tank rolls up, rushes past my Platoon across the street, turns right and stops at the church with its guns right in our back. And then a third comes, but when our PAK starts to shoot he turns round, thank God! Then the enemy infantry starts to come, too. And the day after tomorrow is Christmas Eve.

All this is easily written and reads still more easily. But what one can't describe is all the thoughts that every one of us has in such a situation, and that come up to the surface and have to be put down again, since in these circumstances the lives of hundreds, even thousands of Kameraden could be endangered; the way our men, despite everything, stand there with their MGs in position, simply, quietly, dignified, as they grow beyond and above their own selves, you might even say transfigured—to put all that on paper is simply impossible.

Both enemy tanks are shot by the 3·7, 4·5 and 5 cm. PAK's and burn out. From the first one an officer climbed out and tried to run off; he was promptly knocked off by a dispatch rider from our Company; the second tank ran over a gun-carriage and flattened it out—this was in front of the church—just as the tank started to burn; a Russian jumped out, leaped into a car which was standing there and wanted to take off with it. What an impertinence! We got him, too.

Christmas Eve, 1941

For days now the Russians have been beating against us with a solid, never-ending numerical superiority. It didn't even get as far as man-to-man fights, they didn't even get a chance to yell their 'Hurreeeee' in our ears. We are lying on the eastern bank of the Tim, without any security, and turn them back, to flight. We are holding on.

Day after day, night after night we sit in the open air, and a rain of artillery and small arms fire pours over us. We think our feet will freeze at any moment. And we've no real billets. We are *standing* (!)—30 of us—in a room 3 × 5 metres. No windows. Nor can we heat the place, lest the smoke disclose our whereabouts. But our men—they go on standing. They can't be beaten. It is an act of heroism even greater than that of the World War. It is the most fabulous epoch of German soldiery!

We never dreamt that Christmas Eve would be like this. In the early hours of the morning, at 4.00 o'clock, the Russians attacked our right wing. With their usual 'Hurreeee's' they reached the first houses. The fight went on for a long time, but at last they were turned back. It is quite clear: they are doing this to annoy us, attacking us on Christmas Eve.

I lay the whole day with my Platoon in our position, and waited till they would come into my section. They would have seen quite a show! They have us under fire—artillery, tanks, heavy mortars—the whole time. In the afternoon everything calms down, and now we can think of organizing a Christmas tree. . . .

Enemy artillery is still shooting at us, also some mortars. Will they attack again today? In the evening we stand round the tree and sing some Christmas carols. Songs from home. Fighting songs. Each of us is at home with his thoughts. I imagine what your Christmas Eve is like. It hurts so, Henny. At 22.00 I make the rounds of my alarm and listening posts. The night is still. The snow falls silently. For an hour my thoughts are all with you. . . .

Silent Night, Holy Night

The shock we received a few days ago when the Russian tanks broke through has long since disappeared, and forgotten are the difficult defensive battles of the past days—for today is Christmas Eve!

Will the Russians come a second time today? The enemy artillery shells continually whine over our heads, tear into the earth behind us and explode, spreading about death and destruction. Without pause shells from the Russian heavy mortars crash over our huts, and their splinters sing through the air, looking for victims. The Russian tanks bark from their emplacements, and often a Russian tank shell comes dangerously near.

We have four wounded today, in some the shell fragments are still lodged in the wound, in the others it's a clean wound. We are fighting a desperate defensive battle against an icy Russian winter, against an enemy who have become beasts. Christmas Eve? . . . Is there much time to think of this day, on which our beloved land is celebrating the most German of all holidays, is there time to think of the wonder of the coming night?

Perhaps, however, this 24th of December means specially much to us now, as we stand between death, destruction, night and darkness here and life, happiness, light and joy at home; perhaps it is we, more than all the others, who can comprehend the meaning of this divine rebirth. Slowly time passes, and at last darkness falls.

The quarter-master-noncom brings up mail (I got three letters but no parcels), cognac, chocolate, cakes and cigarettes; one of our people has fixed up a willow branch . . . two candles . . . two apples . . . two stars . . . four red mushrooms with white polka dots . . . a little bell and some tinsel which arrived some time ago in one of the Christmas parcels—that is our Christmas tree.

About 30 men, we stand in our small, cold, draughty hut (not enough room to sit). . . . It is dark now. . . . We light the tree . . . and then someone raises his voice, and we all join in, singing . . . Christmas carols.

Perhaps you, my dear Henny, are at this moment lighting a lovely tree, the thick green of which will be broken by sparkling and glittering; and the next moment you'll be calling the children to come in, to show them that the Christ child has been there. And Hannelore, like last year, will stand in front of the wonderful tree of light with her mouth open and eyes shining, not knowing what she ought to say; while Heinz won't be able to take his eyes off so much light, without knowing what it is because he's too small. And then Hannelore will trot with her presents to Mother, and from there to Father, and then to your parents, and you'll all of you rejoice in her childish delight. . . .

All these last days you will have been expecting me—I wrote saying I was coming on Christmas Eve—and even this morning you won't have given up hope, nor at noon; and it won't be till you light the tree that you finally realize I won't be coming, that I couldn't desert my duty here in front of the enemy . . . and perhaps you'll have an inkling that I am spending these hours here in a wretched hut with death watching close by.

I do not know if the Russians will attack in the next hours and if I shall come through it safely, I do not know if an enemy shell will land the next instant on our hut and blow it and the thirty of us to smithereens . . . but I do know that you will bear my being far off courageously, and that our hearts and our love will be the purer and cleaner for it. You have the children, conceived in the happiest hours of our lives; look in their happy, shining eyes today and you will be happy and proud of your soldiers, who are enabling the children to have this joy. Think of the many women who have lost their husbands, of the children whose fathers rest somewhere in foreign soil, of the mothers whose sons will never return. They have much sorrow to bear.

I know, too, that you will feel the profundity and holiness of this night as fervently as I—more fervently than ever before. And I know that when the bells today proclaim peace, peace on earth, that you too will dream of the peace in which I believe and for which I am fighting. For what is in fact peace? In the usual sense of the word, it means for me: when the danger of death is past, when the guns are silent, when I lay down my weapon; for you: when you no longer need fear for my life, when you no longer need tremble whether I return or not, when you can again sleep quietly these many nights. But surely that cannot be the real, the great peace. For there can never be peace, even if the guns are silent, when the people are constantly fearing that they may be attacked. The true, the real peace, the shining, glowing, joyous peace can only come from this our holy war. I know full well how great, how painful are the sacrifices that those near and dear to us must bear; but they are sacrifices which are made for something which, after all, has meaning.

We have seen the so-called peace that lasted 25 years. It was a stinking and dirty peace, a lying peace which made beasts out of men. We should have had such a peace still, were it not for this truly sacred war. Could our two children be just as happy without this war? I doubt it. And so at 22.00 I go out into the cold, clear December night, wading through the deep snow . . . from post to post . . . into the advance lines . . . and my thoughts are even more intimately with you than before . . . at home . . . and with tears in my eyes I look up to the stars and think I see two pairs of shining, happy children's eyes there . . . and dream with a proud but hurting heart of the miracle of this silent, holy night.

If the Russians attack today, not one of them will come out of it alive. A cold fury is in us now. And, if we think a little deeper and more carefully, a certain pride; for it is because of us that millions of others can celebrate this, the most German of all holidays, in peace and security.

Thursday, 25th December 1941

An icy snowstorm whistles about our ears. The heavy weapons

and machines and the heavy munition packs are a terrible burden to our men and they can only move forward bent way over. In a long column we move westwards along the railway line.

Retreat! It's not a thing to our liking, for we are attackers, we are the ones always and tirelessly pressing forward; we really don't know what the word means. And so our column drags itself along, wordlessly, in the knee-deep snow. Often a box of ammunition has to be left behind because the man is too weak to carry it so far. Thirty kilometres is a long stretch. At every break, each of us drops half dead in the snow, and when we go on, each of us is more tired than before.

Friday, 26th December 1941

At 04.00 we arrive at Ivanovka, soaked through, frozen, exhausted—more dead than alive. I can well imagine that it's the fact of retreating, too, which depresses everyone. Many of us have foot trouble. Myself, I'm completely knocked out with my frost blisters.

It's obvious that there are no quarters for us. I and my Platoon find a cold room. But that's enough; all we want is to find some place to sit and we're satisfied.

We really can't take another march like this one. Everyone is talking of the rumour that we'll be relieved in January. We can hardly go on as it is. For the most part the men have only what they carry on their bodies. Everything else was lost in the retreat, or burned, or the Russians have it. And if you've only got the socks you are wearing, and they are constantly soaked through, in time they'll start to rot. All our shoes are ruined, our shirts and underclothes black (they've not been changed for weeks)—this is just a little hint of the way things are. It's impossible, being without any washing or shaving equipment.

WINTER, 1941–1942

Winter, 1941/1942

[*Printed clipping, probably from an Austrian newspaper*]

Für Führer, Volk und Vaterland
Born 21st April 1914, died 15th September 1941
Mein Lebensspruch war: Ich habs gewagt!
Und ich hoffe nur, dass Frau und Kind,
Die mir das Liebste gewesen sind,
Aufrecht bleiben und unverzagt
Und mit Stolz die Namen der Toten nennen,
Deren Glück war: Deutschland zu bekennen
Und seiner Ehre Kämpfer sein![1]

ᛋᛋ *Ustuf*[2] *Helmut Frischenschlager, Lieutenant in an Alpine Fighter Regiment.*

Frau Annemarie Frischenschlager, née Oswalder, Salzburg, Heinrich-Haubner-Strasse 2.

[*Prüller's comments:*]

In your best, most hopeful years you laid down your life in the fight against Bolshevism. I knew you not, Helmut Frischenschlager, you never crossed the path of my life. For me you are one of the many nameless warriors who gladly and proudly gave their all for our wonderful and everlasting people, for our adored Führer and for this beautiful Germany. It was only through this little clipping that my notice was drawn to you.

Surely your life led you through the difficult political fight, and perhaps you had to pay for your adherence to the German ideal with prison.[3] *Surely, too, you suffered under the economic*

[1] My life's watchword was: I dared! And I only hope that wife and child, who are my dearest, will remain faithful and fearless, and will speak with pride the names of the dead whose fortune it was to profess themselves Germans and to fight for her honour.

[2] Untersturmführer, an SS rank about the equivalent of Lieutenant.

[3] Prüller is referring to the period before 1938, when it was illegal to be a member of the Nazi party in Austria.

conditions that allowed no happiness in our whole country, and you, too, had your own personal victory in the March days of the year 1938.

Thus your life was enriched by the highest and purest idealism, and from your earliest youth, your fight was for the German future. And when the Führer called us to the last and most decisive deed, surely you were one of the first to take up arms, joyfully and enthusiastically, in the fight for your people's, your children's lives.

And now you gave your life, so full of promise, at the age of 27; you gave it in the most loyal fulfilment of duty for Volk, Führer and Vaterland, probably during an attack at the head of your troops. You have won the most beautiful death a man can have, death on the battlefield. But you have not died; for all those whom you have fathered round you will always remember you as the best and most faithful Kamerad. He dies only who dies without honour, but he who dies honourably, lives. You, Helmut Frischenschlager, who have given your life for the highest ideal, you shall be eternal, for you have fallen as a hero for your country, and for the greatness of your fatherland.

Shall I tell you how thankful to you the whole German people are, shall I tell you how very much we sympathize with your wife and child? Give them both into our keeping, and the people will never desert them.

Your grave is perhaps in the fruitful Ukraine, perhaps in the industrial region of the Donets River circle, perhaps in the far north in one of the thick woods of Russia; I know it not, but nevertheless as your Kamerad I must do one more favour for you. It shall be the last: in spirit, I decorate your grave with the most beautiful flowers there are, with the finest Edelweiss from your beloved Salzburg mountains.

So fare thee well, Helmut Frischenschlager, and may you rest peacefully in the foreign soil.

Thursday, 1st January 1942

During the past days—quite often in the nights, too—the Russians attacked, but were beaten back. They advanced in such a silly way that the whole thing looked more like a demonstration than an attack. They would stop on the incline, apparently to rest, and made a wonderful target for our artillery. And after the first few shots they would disappear over the brow of the hill again, running like stuck pigs.

So it was today. At first we thought it was their revenge for our New Year's barrage yesterday: at 00.00 we shot off every gun we had at them, using every kind of munition. They may have thought we had left, but we taught them differently.

The snow is very deep, and it's cold—often 35 or 40 degrees below zero [centigrade]. But we must put up with it.

Saturday, 3rd January 1942

Yesterday I had such a frightful toothache that at 22.00 I went to the first-aid station and wanted them to pull the tooth by the light of a petroleum lamp. Unfortunately that didn't work, but they gave me a terrific powder, and that helped till this morning. I should go to Shchigry, but I can't go even for a moment until things quieten down here.

The whole time now, day and night, there have been countless alarms. The Russians often came in droves, at times it was only a scouting party, often it was only a false alarm; the latter happens when one of the sentries has a green (instead of a white) Verey light, or a whistling rocket, in his Verey light pistol, and shoots the thing without first checking what he loaded it with. I could shoot an idiot like that, especially when it happens at night, but you can't let yourself go, of course. It's just what we learned as recruits. A lot—in fact most things—you only learn by drilling, crawling on your stomach, getting punished or having your leave taken away: unfortunately no way to teach them during a war.

Sunday, 4th January 1942

We are to change our position again. A few kilometres to the right where we are to relieve the 2nd Company, who in turn are to go farther to the right. We find the billets aren't bad, each troop has its own house. The civilians are still here, too, which is a great help. In Ivanovka, I picked up a nice dog, who had been lying for days—perhaps even for weeks—in a barn. I called him Ivan: he ran away from me twice, but I always managed to get him again.

I hope that this will be our permanent winter quarters. We could stick it here. This part of the front isn't bad either; the Russians can come and attack us here if they want to—they'll see what happens!

Wednesday, 7th January 1942

Today I shaved off my 'protest' beard. I couldn't stand looking at myself any longer.

Friday, 9th January 1942

Today the C.O. suggested my name for the Iron Cross, 1st Class!

23rd January 1942

I have just learned that all leaves have been cancelled for the whole Wehrmacht. Probably the deployment for the offensive has started rolling; and with it we hope that we'll be relieved. I expect this to happen about the end of March.

30th January 1942

For days now we've been having a huge snowstorm. The thermometer often drops to 43 degrees below zero [centigrade]. It's quite beyond praise what our listening posts, often way out in front on heights lashed by the snow and wind, go through, also the scouting patrols, who climb about the whole night in no-man's-land.

Time is working for us now. Every day. New reserves are

coming up, new troop concentrations (they don't get to us!), so that it wouldn't be such a mess if the Russians broke through now. All the rumours that we are to be relieved in March and be moved to the south of France get stronger all the time. It was even talked of recently at one of the C.O.'s teas. March! That would be only eight more weeks.

1st February 1942

This winter is terribly hard. And it can go on a good 6 or 8 weeks. It's simply a miracle the way the supply and munition people work. No vehicle can get from here to Shchigry—that's seven kilometres. No horse wagons either, because the animals sink up to their rumps in the drifts. No sleighs, either. And yet everything arrives. Not even the railway between Kursk and S. is open, but everything moves like a well oiled clock. The miracle of German organization again! I wonder though if we shall ever see anything of the winter uniforms, furs, wool things, &c., which people donated back home. Actually, we've managed to get through the winter all right up to now. If it doesn't get a lot worse, we can take it.

11th February 1942

If anyone had said to me in the summer that we would spend the winter in Russia, I would have said he was mad. We, an armoured division, who have been at the front the whole time, without vehicles and defending the whole winter? I would have bet anything that this wouldn't be possible.

And now February is almost finished, the winter is nearly at an end, and here we still are! Moreover, we've stood it marvellously up to now. The cold doesn't bother us any more, we've got used to it. Thirty-eight degrees or 40 degrees below? That's nothing. The worst was 43 degrees below.

The two retreats we went through were really very shitty, but now we can understand better the morale of the Russians when they are chased hundreds of kilometres, often without food and without any hope whatever of getting in the ring again. We pulled back 40 km. and were quite desperate. And we've held fast for weeks now: the front is solid now.

12th February 1942

Wind, rain and warm weather has set in now. It's certainly not the end of the winter, but it's a sign that spring can't be far off. And then we'll roll on again, towards the east. Whether we'll be with them isn't clear as yet, but whether it's we or others the enemy will be chased, encircled, beaten, destroyed. Stalin and Co. will be awaiting the spring with horror. It'll be the beginning of the end for them.

England will fall. A long time ago the Führer made this prophetic announcement. Are there better days than now to confirm these three words? The Philippines, Hong Kong, Singapore, Burma, Borneo, Java, Celebes, Sumatra! The empire is cracking, breaking up. A whole kingdom will fall. And not National Socialism. That's the way the cards lie. What does it matter, our getting leave, being relieved, or no leave and further advance? The victory must be ours. All of us must serve this goal: every last man!

We've got our own tame house-partisan girl, who comes every day at 08.00 and works till 17.00. She never had food like that which our kitchen provides.

14th February 1942

Today orders came to have the civilians evacuated—for the umpteenth time. Probably somebody at the top level got the bright idea that we could be lapping up all the available food ourselves if the civilians weren't there.

Well, that order has been in effect a long while, but the inhabitants always returned, we quietly allowed this; for they heat for us, fetch water, wash for us, even bring milk from the two cows—well, and after all among the 230 men there are some who can't stand it without having female flesh about, even if it's

Russian flesh. And so after a time we had them all over our necks.

Now the Herr General has put through the order himself. There isn't very much we can do to get out of it now. But the order was carried out as follows: the Herr Bataillonskommandeur allowed that each Company could keep three families who were to be used for work, and that each member of the family was to receive a permit signed by the Company C.O. Three families? That's not very much in relation to the needs of a Company. But: *we* put the families together ourselves! Nine inhabitants—men and wife—are included in one family, they all get their permit and each of them is called Ivanov. The next nine are called Baranova; and the others Vassiliev.

23rd February 1942

A long time ago a letter to an unknown soldier of the Company arrived in which a girl asked to have information about her dead fiancé. No one wanted to answer it, because there's no one here any more who was there when he fell. Thus the letter wandered about from one to the other till it finally landed in my lap. I wrote her the following letter:

Dear Mitzi Trunka,

After various detours I received your letter to an unknown soldier of the Feldpost No. 13694; no one dared to answer it. And I can't really blame anyone, for none of the Kameraden who were near your fiancé when he met his hero's death is with the Company any more. He fell on 4th August in the great battle of Uman, as the Company was attacking Ternovka, and lies buried with other Kameraden who fell there in Tishkovka, 50 km. north-east of Uman. A shot in the lung robbed him of his life at the very height of his power. The death was immediate and without pain.

Believe me, Fräulein Trunka, that I understand only too well how much you miss your beloved fallen man. But you are a German girl; and as such you are as enthusiastic about our fight for the life or death of our people as all of us who are here on the front. Later in your life, in a quiet hour, when you have your own family, you will remember with thanks beyond measure all the victims which this gigantic battle has demanded, and will demand. It is they, and only they, who will have saved us and our children from a life of degradation and shame, of distress and desperation.

I know that it is easy to speak of the sacrifice which the relatives of those who fell must take upon themselves, when one does not have to bear the brunt oneself; but as I think, so does each of us here. And every one of us is sure that the grain that is sown will one day be reaped.

Just as we here are proud to have taken part in this great fight, so you, Fräulein Trunka, must be proud to have made such a heavy sacrifice for this fight. It was not, it shall not be in vain! Your Martin shall also be avenged! The survival of our great Fatherland, our imperishable people, and the victory over our accursed enemies shall have been accomplished partly through his death.

In our remembrance of the fallen Kameraden left behind I include you too, Fräulein Trunka; and greet you in sincere sympathy.

Long live the Führer!
Prüller.

26th February 1942

After a cold day, snow and wind have set in again; immediately all the roads are full of drifts, the streets impassable. Let's hope that these are winter's last throes. We have finally received official confirmation—from Battalion—that we shall be pulled out of here in April. We are supposed to go back to Germany or Roumania and rest, and then to go to Turkey. It doesn't matter where so long as it's far away from this Russia. And back home again? That would be the best of all.

Yesterday three deserters from the farm-house opposite us came over. The morale over there is very low; most of them would like to desert, but the commissar is standing behind them.

They get little food, and that at rare intervals, but plenty of munition. Most of them are from penal colonies with ten or more years in front of them, and they are badly trained and equipped. A funny set-up. Well, it doesn't matter so long as they keep quiet.

Whatever the commissars tell them, they believe almost entirely: that we're about to collapse, that we're starving, that we would run like rabbits if they attacked, that we shoot all prisoners, that the Russians have 26 batteries (!) in Leshinki, that an armoured battalion of the Russians is advancing, etc., etc., etc. They're so silly! If they only dreamt what's going to happen to them in a few weeks!

Today we got a new gun, with a barrel out of cardboard. Don't laugh, it's *really* made out of cardboard. And it shoots, too—as far as two kilometres. The bullets are propaganda bombs which comprise more than 100 leaflets; at 2,000 metres, about 1·5 metres above the earth, they are spread all over the earth. Isn't that fabulous?

An important factor in this war thus appears on the horizon: propaganda. And in that respect, too, we beat the Russians, in fact we're miles ahead of them. We've got a Goebbels, after all!

The mail is working, at least more or less, again; of course we're never satisfied with it and always think it could be improved.

16th March 1942

In the night of the 12th and 13th a snowstorm began and went on till this morning. We'd never seen anything like it. You couldn't see ten steps. If you had to go from one hut to the other, it was a real fight to get there. The huts were snowed in, right to the straw roofs.

In our hole it was so cold that we stood round the stove in furs—fur hats and ear muffs, gloves, two or three blankets and a fur; and it was still so cold you couldn't stand it. The wind whistled through the nooks and crannies and it was grim. It was a real Russian winter. If that had gone on for a few weeks, it would have been a pretty mess. And today everything was normal again. Our supplies, and even the long-awaited mail, is to arrive, and in Shchigry they will have mail tomorrow, also tidbits (Schnaps, cigarettes, &c.). How *do* they do it?

17th March 1942

The news at 22.00 brought us a tremendous surprise. The Führer has given our C.O. the Ritterkreuz. Nobody expected it, because he just got the German Cross in gold a little while ago. He didn't expect it either. We were all terribly pleased. And all the telephone calls with congratulations simply wouldn't stop. At 24.00 we listened to the news again . . . 'Oberleutnant Hans Henning Eichert received the Ritterkreuz of the Eisernen Kreuzes. . . .' Quite obvious that the quartermaster produced a bottle from his 'very last reserve'. We had to celebrate this. Now we're waiting for the oak clusters. . . .

March 1942

Does he who lies the most, win?

We experienced the lies of the Polish Government. With our own ears, when we were prisoners, we heard the way they persuaded their soldiers that the Germans were surrendering in regiments, that we were deserting, divisions at a time. And we saw how they sang their National Anthem for joy over the news. This was going on between 22nd and 25th September, when there wasn't any more Polish army, when they were being destroyed in their own traps, or being taken prisoner. And they were convinced that they would beat the Germans and would be marching into Berlin in a short while. And they did not win!

We heard the daily French news broadcasts in the German language—it was forbidden, but we kept getting the Paris Radio because we were already in France and our apparatus was too weak to pick up German stations. Every evening we heard the words: 'Germans! Give up this useless, fruitless fight. Your sons are falling before the deadly sweep of our machine-guns as the wheat stalk falls before the scythe. Mountains of corpses are piled up in front of our emplacements. France's soil is soaked in the blood of your dead, Germans!' Every day at the same time the same monotonous words.

Holland capitulated, and Belgium. Dunkirk occurred; we broke out of the Amiens bridgehead and drove the enemy before us. And still the lies of Radio Paris went on. In the very night when German soldiers marched into the capital of France: lies, lies. And the French did not win.

When our divisions, in a bold thrust, broke through the Köstendil region and three days later reached Usküb[1] *and the Albanian border, thus cutting off the Serbian Southern Army, the Serbs sent their lies into the world: they are stronger than ever, the German armies are being constantly pushed back, the losses on the German side run into the hundreds of thousands, the booty in weapons and munitions is reaching unheard-of numbers . . . and . . . and . . . and the Serbs did not win.*

We then stood at the Aliakmon, at the Stena Portas, in the middle of the worst battles for Greece; and the Greeks threw English, Australian and New Zealand troops at us in the most difficult sort of terrain, and they held us up for a few days and then lied that the German advance had been stopped. The Greek Macedonian Army gave up ('The Germans are being beaten on all fronts'), on Mount Olympus the German battle flag was hoisted ('The Front is now stationary'), we moved down from Mount Olympus ('the Germans were thrown back'). And they were still lying when we got through the Stena Portas and were pursuing the enemy in a relentless chase through Larissa and into Pharsala. And they did not win.

And now we have been nearly a year in Russia, and have heard the worst lies of all. I don't say this because of the bolshevistic system: the case against that's been proved, and the whole civilized world has meanwhile seen that communism is one huge legal swindle, one huge, infamous lie. I merely want to speak of the lies which concern our fight here for the decent world. I shall select

[1] Or Skoplje.

only a few, for several tomes would not be sufficient to incorporate all the Russian lies.

They say, of course, that we are deserting in thousands; that the prisoner-of-war camps are not large enough to take in all the diverse German divisions; that we are fleeing from the Third Reich and want to trumpet the blessings of the Soviet paradise to the whole world—these are the more harmless lies. But when the wireless and Press here and abroad scream their protest and disgust at our treatment of Russian prisoners and the Russian civilian population, when they lie about bestial murders and mutilation—that gets more interesting. For we have been able to persuade ourselves on hundreds of occasions that exactly the opposite obtains. And our best proof is the prisoners themselves and the population of the part we've occupied, who never were so well off in their whole lives, who never even heard of such a treatment as described above, whose existence changed 180 degrees after 22nd June 1941. These men and women, whether prisoners or not, see this 'bestiality' of ours for themselves in the course of several months. They are the witnesses of the excellent behaviour of the German Wehrmacht, they are the best propagandists for the German way of life in Russia. But Stalin goes on lying. . . .

Do I need to repeat that not one German soldier has even touched a Russian woman?[1] *That is quite obvious. How can they believe over there that we are not aware what German honour, morals and discipline mean in this respect? It is simply an impertinence to lie that we have anything to do with these basically filthy sluts. Over there they don't seem to know what a German woman looks like. But Stalin lies about rapings. . . .*

A man who has been a front soldier, and mainly here in the east, knows how rarely we get any alcohol. And when we do get it, it's mostly in tea or coffee. They are very frugal with such things. But then they lie to the Russian soldiers that we, the deutsche Michel, get drunk every Saturday, are unconscious in the night and therefore incapable of resistance the next morning. Prisoners told us this often. But Stalin lies about our Sunday drunkenness. . . .

Many generals came. And failed. Voroshilov, Timoshenko,

[1] See p. 142 for another version.

Budjenny, then came autumn, mud, hunger, revolution, the endless Russian plains, supply problems. And then the greatest general of them all came: winter. And with him, the Russian offensive. And we were supposed to have run like scared rabbits, leaving behind weapons and machines and clothes, frozen in the huge snow-drifts, giving up town after town, and the Russians were tearing after us in a mad offensive—and here we are, months later, still 70 km. east of Kursk, exactly where we were on 26th December 1941. But Stalin lies, and lies. . . .

They all lied. In Poland, in the west, in the Balkans. And not one of them won—not the Poles, not the Dutch, not the Belgians, not the French and the Serbs and the Greeks. And the Russians will not win either!

23rd March 1942

Now we are to have leave! For how long, when, &c. will be told us today. We may send three men. I'm one of them, because I got the short end of the stick at Christmas, as the C.O. says. Hurrah! Perhaps I shall be home for Easter! That would be the best Easter gift!

Semenovka–Vienna–Semenovka.[1]

On 27th March 1942—after being postponed for two days (it wouldn't be complete without this army gesture!)—it really happened: I went on leave.

What did I care about the five-hour trip from Shchigry to Kursk in an open lorry, what did I care about my temperature of 39 degrees (about 100 degrees)? My only thoughts were at home. They all sent me off with the best wishes and were very happy for me, some of course with heavy hearts, for naturally everyone wants to go home. . . .

I bitch often and in my own way, and like every soldier I curse a lot—that's even allowed—and my usual saying is: 'typical army'. But on this trip home—the delousing in Przemysl and the way

[1] Prüller wrote this section in May, and in another volume. We have placed it here, in its proper chronological position.

everything was organized—we were all terrifically impressed. Everything, but everything, was fabulously prepared and just as magnificently carried out.

No wonder that we were in the best of moods, if a bit more quiet than usual. It's quite a thing when after 14 months you are to meet your dearest and the children. It's like a dream. I paint to myself the first moment of reunion, the first evening in my nice little flat, the children . . . and in Lundenburg I cannot yet believe that in two hours I shall be standing in front of my own name on the door. How shall I ring the bell? Quickly and hesitatingly? Or long and stormily? Will I take my dear, brave wife and the children in my arms, filled with utter joy, or will I stand in the doorway, incapable of saying a word? I don't know. I keep looking at my watch and counting the kilometres which bring me nearer to my goal.

How lovely this German land is, how clean the houses, fields and roads, how completely different the people, in dress and clothing, in character and ability. One simply has *to be proud to be a German.*

Slowly the radio towers on the Bisamberg approach, now you can recognize Leopoldsberg and Kahlenberg. We cross the Danube. From the windows of the houses, from the street-cars, from the huge factory windows, where people crowd to wish us welcome, to call to us, to wave at us. Before I quite realize that I have arrived in my home city, the train rolls into the Nordwestbahnhof. I must confess that a stolen tear of joy ran down my cheek and that it was hard to choke back the lump in my throat. Home . . . Vienna . . . I can scarcely believe it.

We are all pressing towards the exit. Everyone wants to get out as quickly as possible. A few friendly greetings can be heard, and then . . . then I'm pushed out on the street. Hesitatingly and uncertainly I look round . . . the Praterstern . . . it's all so new, the traffic, the paved streets, the tall houses, the people, the women. Drunk with happiness, I take in the shape of the city, during the street-car ride I let it flow past my eyes. The passengers look at me curiously: can they see that I come from Russia, from the eastern front? Why of course, I am still wearing the Russian fur hat I captured. Off with it at once, and on with my field cap.

In this atmosphere of unreality I cross the little market-square near my flat. It's market time. Will my wife even be home? What shall I do if she isn't? I have no key. Then I throw away such thoughts.

Steps behind me turn into running. Instinctively I turn round . . . and . . . take my wife into my arms. . . .

Oh you wonderful, you magical leave. Twenty-one heavenly days. Every one a festival. Impossible to describe them. The family circle, undimmed by any worry, the playing—hours at a time—with the children, the chatting with your wife, the exchange of experiences, the stories, this 'being together again' . . . it was all too marvellous.

After all the misery and unhappiness, after the privations and exhaustion, after all those months in which we did without any kind of civilization: three weeks at home. No more sleeping in holes, no lice, no alarm, no attacks. That wasn't only a leave—it can't be more lovely in Heaven, surely: a soft white bed, pyjamas, running water—when it gets dark, you press a tiny button and there is bright, streaming light; every day a paper, the wireless and . . . peace. Ah, there are a thousand details, normally impossible to do without, but missed since 22nd June.

And then I am standing with a mass of parcels for my Kameraden, for my Company C.O., on the Nordbahnhof, at the train which will again take me to the east. A quick kiss and a firm handclasp—that was all for a good-bye; but in this handclasp were more than a thousand words—in them were the past, the present, the future . . . in them was Germany!

Slowly the train moves out of the station, past mothers, wives, fiancées, fathers, brothers, those many who stood beside the slowly moving train, waving, tears rolling down their cheeks; how many of them have a strange presentiment that from those in this train, many will remain out there? . . . Perhaps their loved one, too.

My wife remained brave to the end. The train rolled across the Danube bridge, and my thoughts already turn to the front, to my Kameraden.

29th April 1942

At noon I got back from leave and reported to the Company.

20th May 1942

For some days now we have been having a near tropical heat-wave. We're running round in bathing-trunks.

3rd June 1942

Today the C.O. of the new unit arrived. The infantry is to take over our positions in the night, and we are to leave tomorrow morning. We were five months in Semenovka—with many attacks, many small victories. We stood it, our first Russian winter. Will there be another? These huts and bunkers, these trenches, they were our home during this period. None of us can ever forget this hole. Despite all the difficulties, we felt well here—it was *our* place. And thus we take leave with curiously mixed feelings.

19th June 1942

Big excitement for days now. We've been anxiously waiting, for since Monday we were supposed to move to our troop concentration-rendezvous. But it seems that the weather has put a spanner in the works, for it's rained without stopping for some time now. And anyone can picture the way the roads look—one single sea of mud. So it will certainly take some time before we go into action. We are reported to be the first unit which will advance.

22nd June 1942

It can only be a matter of days before we go into action. What's moving on our road alone is something fantastic—column upon column, artillery, infantry, new weapons (are they smoke mortars?), supply—without pause. On every road and cart-track.

23rd June 1942

We are filled with a proud, thankful emotion, for again we are to be the first to leap at the Soviets. At last we are again in our element, as attackers, as breathless pursuers. Thus it is we who are taking the initiative, Mr. Stalin. And neither you nor your beasts can stop us. The coming days will prove it.

If only the weather is good to us.

27th June 1942

If no orders to the contrary arrive before 18.00, the operation begins tonight. A burst of fire from the heavy guns—supposedly at 02.15—will give the sign for us to cross the Tim River. The dinghies are already lying in camouflaged positions and will be brought by Pioneers to the river's edge. Everyone has to rush across the Tim in double quick time, of course, and we have as our first target Nish. Dolgoe, as our second the edge of Gratschewka and as our third the heights to the south.

It is a warm moonlit night. The men up front move as silently as cats, and the 8.8 flak boys push their gun just as silently into position. Occasionally a noncom swears at one of his men when he lights a cigarette too carelessly, but otherwise the silence is almost corpselike.

To the right of us are two large red stone buildings. They stand on the Tim, lonely, and don't fit in at all, right in the middle of the countryside—they were once schools. Between the bushes you can see, here and there, the small glittering band which is the Tim. Tim! End of the year 1941, beginning of the year 1942! How much blood has flowed along your banks in the last half year! How often have you changed owners? Soon the change will be permanent, however, and no Russian soldier will ever shoot on your banks.

Sunday, 28th June 1942

At 02.15 the artillery corps let off their first shot, and in that same instant, as the shell was winging its way towards the Russian installations, the heavy guns start a barrage the like of which none of us in the whole Battalion has ever heard before. Guns of every sort and calibre, batteries without number, spew their deadly shells at the enemy bank. The 8·8 flak barks, the 2 cm. flak chatters, the heavy mortars roar, the artillery thunders— all in rapid-fire confusion. In between, the bombs of our new weapon howl—the rocket mortars[1] (something like our 'Stuka zu Fuss').

In the midst of this roar, the men are crossing the Tim with their little rafts in feverish haste. We are attacking on a broad front: many, many divisions are moving simultaneously across the Tim. Hundreds of thousands can now move again after the banishment of the winter, can move eastwards; we are so happy about it.

I'm still on this side of the Tim, clearing the Platoons so they can cross quickly at the appointed time. When the last Platoon hits the rafts, I rush into the water, and jump into one, already overfilled; but before I can even grasp what's happening, I'm on the other side.

The Companies are still lying in a protected position. We collect everyone and then move off towards Nish. Dolgoe, a village about 1½ km. from here; its capture is our first point of attack. The land is bathed in a thick fog, because of the many mortar, artillery and bomb hits, as well as the smoke-screen. You can't recognize anything at 20 feet.

All about us is still an ear-splitting, gigantic racket, shot after shot, the scream of rockets kicked off by rocket mortars, a never-ending inferno. Meanwhile, we've fallen in, stormed across the enemy artillery and mortar fire, got through, as if by a miracle (or was it my nose?) the Soviet minefields, and landed in the middle of a Russian ditch shielded by a row of bushes.

[1] 'Nebelwerfer' (also 'DO-Werfer') was a rocket gun, 15 cm. calibre, six barrels to a gun, six guns to a battery. [S.L.]

It's not easy to know where to make for now, because the fog doesn't allow you any sense of direction: people from another Company run past us—they belong over to the right—infantry tears right through our middle—they belong more towards the left—and at the beginning we are too far to the right ourselves, but during the actual attack we all got to our proper assigned places.

In another ditch which we are using to get out of the enemy fire, we find 70 or 80 Bolsheviks who have to be mowed down, driven off or taken prisoner. A man-to-man fight takes place, and only very few Soviets get away alive. We have some losses too, though: the best and most conscientious young chap I ever met in this war, our medical orderly, Gefreiter Handler, was badly wounded; several other popular men have been knocked out, too. In our neighbour Company the indestructible Lt. Näser fell—a wonderful chap. Now he lies at the Tim. . . .

We reached our first target, Nish. Dolgoe, or rather the place where it used to stand, up till a few hours ago. The few wooden huts were blown to smithereens by our rocket mortars. Tiny remains—a few strong wooden beams and bits of household equipment—are all that's left. Frightened civilians, crawling out of the cellars, the fear of death in their eyes, weeping children, grown-ups shaking with fear, the apathy of the very old ones—that was Nish. Dolgoe. Dear God, we thank Thee that this war must not be fought on German soil.

The next target—Gratschewka—is now before us. First we must get to the south-east entrance. In a broad skirmishing line we attack again, comb the place, and have to use all our combined forces to root out some of the enemy who fight to the end in their fox-holes. But we're moving up fast. On past the Soviets, beaten and marching to the rear, past the dead, past trenches and bunkers, past enemy gun emplacements which they abandoned in an attempt to save their skins . . . we hardly waste a look: on, on, that's the motto.

Across hollows and valleys, over hills and rises, the forward troops wiping out pockets of resistance, and at a gallop we tear across a piece of land raked by enemy fire and reach our second target.

Then on to the third target, the hills south of Uspenskoye. It's only a few metres from there to the railway line Kursk–Voronezh and a few kilometres to Marmyzhi, the scene of such dreadful fighting in the second half of December 1941. How will it look now?

We push on, kilometre after kilometre. The Soviets seem to have withdrawn and as a result of our thrust to the south-east, we are now behind the Soviet echelons. It's oppressively hot, and we are sweaty, dirty, tired, and slowly getting hungry (it must be getting quite late). . . . But on we go, on, on. I find myself remembering the first days of this war in Poland; they were similar. Again some tall wheatfields—I hate them so—have to be crossed. And it's curious (am I being silly?), I keep warning my men about mines, here 10 km. beyond the Tim.

Noon comes. And goes. On, on. . . . Like everything in life, this march has an end, too. After 17 km., at 14.30, we finally reach the heights south of Uspenskoye. Hardly had I discussed all the steps to be taken—the C.O. is with the Battalion Orderly Officer over on the left wing—when it happened.

Suddenly an explosion very near to me. No whining of the shell, no whistling, just the muffled cough of a mortar shell. Is it air pressure or instinct?

In a split second I'm on my belly, just in time for a second explosion. My head roars inside, and I think my ear-drums have burst. What's happened to me? I feel my skull—it's all right. Fine, in fact. Chest—nothing. Hands—nothing. I can move the upper part of my body. Legs—the trousers at the knee are ripped to pieces. Blood comes from the left. I'm wounded.

After three years at the front, after four campaigns, I've got mine.

I could weep with rage. Now, when we're moving again at last, when we could really ram our way eastward, something like this has to happen. Carefully, because I secretly hope that nothing serious has happened, I examine my left leg. Blood is pouring out of the knee. So it's a splinter.

I turn my leg over, but the splinter won't come out, it's sitting inside. Oh-oh! A medical orderly from infantry who got separated from his outfit, and whom I took along with us till he could be sent back *via* Battalion, bandaged me. I can't bend my knee. What will happen? Suddenly the worst thing occurs to me—you'll lose that leg! No, no! Then: it'll be as stiff as a board. Frightful.

After a while Lt. Schemm comes along. He's beside himself. Who shall take my place? I suggest my old Kamerad, Mayer II. Agreed. I have him come to me so that I can explain everything to him.

So: there's Mayer. Well, the daily reports are like this . . . here's my notebook with the leaves for everyone worked out.

'Hey, Prüller, Oberfeldwebel Heindl is wounded too, you can go with him.'

'Yes, yes, just a minute. Now look, here is where the secret stuff is . . . munition . . . the supply. . . .'

'Prüller, come on, will you?'

'The vehicles you'll have to . . . petrol. . . . Now, another thing, you've got to take a scouting party into the woods and . . .'

'Dammit, Prüller, shift your arse over here. . . .'

'Wait a second, for Christ's sake . . . now, don't forget to put in these promotion lists . . . and . . . and . . .' There was so much I should have said.

Lt. Schemm wants to cheer me up, he says the splinter will be removed at the first-aid station and I can stay here with the Company. But I knew what a knee splinter meant. A Steyr is all ready for us, with two other wounded men aboard—Heindl and Pfc. Töpl from our 4th Platoon. With the medical orderly's help I manage to limp a few steps, then I'm through.

With a painful twist in my heart, I take leave of this wonderful Kameradschaft, in which I was bound to this Company for 3½ years, I take leave of the front. Shall I experience it again? God be with you, my dear 6th, may soldier's luck be with you always.

The main first-aid station is set up in several large tents. It takes some time till my turn comes. I get a real deal—my leg in a splint and one injection against tetanus and a shot of morphine against the pain. Then I'm taken to one of the large tents to await evacuation to the rear.

29th June 1942

It was an awful night. The splint allowed me to sleep only on my back, and in that position I can't sleep. Enemy bombers worked over us the whole night. Some bombs dropped dangerously near to us. That would be the ticket, to be wounded again here! Heindl, who had numerous splinters extracted, bears his pain with admirable calm.

Next to me is a *Feldwebel* from the 377th Infantry. He has a shot in the chest and lies in his own vomit. It has been raining since yesterday evening, and there's no hope of our getting away. The ambulance would get stuck in Shchigry, and that's 40 or 45 km. away. Thank God, I've still some cigarettes.

30th June 1942

Today we're supposed to leave in the early hours. If this proves to be true, I shall write it up later.

Later. That was a frightful trip from here to Shchigry. The huge holes in the roads kept making the vehicle rock, and we inside were more in the air than on our stretchers. We kept yelling 'ow' at him, but the driver couldn't do anything but keep going at that tempo; otherwise we would have got stuck in the mud. We were relieved to get to the Army Hospital at S., but we weren't even taken out of the ambulance; they took down our particulars right on the street, and then sent us off to the station. A provisional hospital train—goods wagons with some straw on the floor—was standing on the tracks ready to leave. For Kursk. When we got there, on to Konotop. In Konotop, it was on to Gomel.

My knee hurts rather a lot, and in the night I took off the splint; but then I couldn't stand it. The trip seemed endless. Some of us were taken off in Kursk, others in Konotop. They were so badly wounded, the poor things, that they couldn't have stood the trip any further. Finally we arrived at Gomel at noon of 2nd July. There we were taken on stretchers to the Casualty Collecting Centre which is right at the station. Our bandages were changed, and the next day we were off again, in another provisional hospital train—but much better than before. We had straw sacks, at least, and a nurse in each car. The Red Cross took care of us at every station. We could not possibly eat and smoke everything they gave us.

On 5th July we arrived in Warsaw. They took me to the hospital in the Dobrastrasse. Right away we got deloused and bathed (that was marvellous). They gave me a new splint, much more comfortable than the old one. I felt as if I had been reborn: lying, washed, in a clean white bed, fresh linen, a wireless set in the room, attentive nurses—it was like a dream.

The X-ray pictures showed that the splinter was in two sections, and both the little things are stuck in my bones. I don't have any more pain, but I can't sleep—the damn splint.

Our stay in Warsaw, as planned, was not for long. As soon as you are capable of being moved, you go to Germany in a hospital train. The first time I had to give in—the train was going to Dresden. Meanwhile the splint was removed and I got a plaster cast. A day later I had to prepare to leave, and on the 9th in the evening I was on a train bound for the right destination—Vienna!

In the night of the 11th we arrived in Vienna at the Aspangbahnhof. The next morning at 08.00 we were taken off, and when I got my hospital orders I almost fainted—Boltzmanngasse in the 9th District, ten minutes from my home! I managed to get the ambulance (it was one of the Vienna city vehicles) to go past my house and let my wife know I had arrived.

They decided not to operate, otherwise my knee would have remained stiff. Whether I shall ever regain its full use is doubtful; time will tell.

On the 30th (July) I received an airmail letter from Battalion, in which I was informed that I had been decorated with the Iron Cross 1st Class. On 1st August I went out for the first time. I could barely move my knee.

The Führer Speaks

December 1942[1]

We had just set up the safety posts in Vesseloye, which we had taken half an hour before, and then found a hut for ourselves and begun to fix it up for the night. Probably we shall be moving on tomorrow, thought most of us, but still we put up our wireless set. After a lot of fiddling and fussing we got it going, and turned right away to the Deutschlandsender.[2] *A roar of approval thundered out of the loudspeaker. After we had waited curiously a few seconds the announcer made it clear that the Führer was about to speak. Those who had the time and the desire—and who had* not *the desire?—were rounded up; practically everyone felt they simply had to listen to him.*

And then we sat there on the clay floor and listened to this voice that we love so dearly, our sparkling eyes following his magnificent words. You couldn't have got another pin into the hut, so crowded was it. All of us fastened fascinated eyes on the loudspeaker—as if he would be standing there, the Führer. Although only a few of his sentences could be understood—the Russian jamming was too strong—no one left before the end. Every word was balm to our souls. We couldn't lose one, not a single one. My God! You *know with what buoyancy and verve, with what enthusiasm we shall carry the attack forward to the enemy tomorrow! In each of us the words of the Führer are still ringing.*

Slowly the column crept along. Such a dull trip: the rain slapped against the car's roof, forced its way through the holes and the doors into the inside of our jeep; and when the 'road' was interrupted by a gaping hole, the canvas roof was pushed back and a

[1] Prüller left the hospital on 28th August and went on sick (or rather recovery) leave with his family. During the autumn he remained in or near Vienna—his knee healed very slowly—and he seems to have written this piece while on the so-called 'Hitler-Urlaub' ('Hitler Leave', a special vacation granted to wounded soldiers who had distinguished themselves in battle) at Weitenfeld, near Retz, Lower Austria. The article describes events which took place during the Russian campaign, and has thus been included here.

[2] A powerful Berlin station.

whole sea of rain water poured in on us. It was evening by now. No one spoke a word. Each of us was with his thoughts elsewhere or was busy with this uncomfortable drive. At last someone had the idea of turning on the wireless. Well! The Führer was speaking!

Forgotten the dull trip, forgotten the wretched rain, wetness and cold which had so depressed us. All other thoughts flew away, and devotedly we listened to his words. Every bump disturbed us and we cursed, every noise or changing of gears by the driver earned him a poke in the ribs from the C.O.—we must have reverent silence; for the Führer speaks!

We had been in our permanent winter quarters for a month. At that time I was leading our 2nd Platoon. The C.O. invited all the platoon leaders for coffee and remarked that the Führer was going to speak that day and we could stay and listen.

I arrived at battle headquarters a quarter of an hour beforehand; and then we sat over coffee and sandwiches, and when we had finished, he spoke. . . . Caught up in the enthusiasm with which he built up the party, the state, the people—despite the set-backs—fascinated by his words, by his visionary certainty, at one with him in the certainty of victory, in the vow to do our all for Germany, we leaned back, comfortably and happily, and were as delighted as small children when he scoffed at the other world.

Certainly this Russian winter is almost unbearable, and demands hearts strong and true. But we shall come through it. The Führer has said so!

'Therefore I have decided once again to lay the fate and the future of the German Reich and peoples in the hands of our soldiers.'

And we shall accomplish it, my Führer! No one shall outdo us in faithfulness, obedience and in our belief in you and the ultimate victory! And no one shall shake us in these beliefs, come what may.

'When this war ends, I shall return from it a much more fanatical National Socialist than I was before.'

In so far as we went into this war without being National Social-

ists, in so far as the one or the other of us entered the ring without yet having believed in the Movement, now in this war, in these days of battle, in the hours of enemy fire, even the last man has discarded all foreign things from him and has showed his colours for Germany, for his people, and thus for the Movement too. Not till now can every man measure the blessings of the Reich, not till now can each one of us understand the extent of our debt of gratitude to you, my Führer, and to the Movement, for our salvation, for the coming victory and for the future of our people.

'The supreme courage shown at the front is immortal, and for such an immortal deed we who believe, as people, in Providence may assume that the reward will be everlasting.'

Reward? My Führer, we thirst not after reward! We thirst after victory! And if you, my Führer, are satisfied with us, with the deeds of us soldiers; and if you not only recognize it but draw special attention to it, that is the finest reward we can have. More than that we really do not want: for we are already so unspeakably proud, so incredibly well rewarded!

How superior we feel after each one of the Führer's speeches! How full of enthusiasm we are for this difficult battle! How intensely we believe in the victory! How sure of it we are after each of the Führer's speeches! The Führer speaks, and all listen—the entire country at home, the whole of Europe, yes, the whole world! But do not we—his soldiers—perhaps understand him best?

While we look at the loudspeaker in silent concentration, breathing in his fortifying words as if they were the Gospel; while we drink in his sentences, each one so logical, so utterly convincing; while we are being swept away by his speech—as by nothing else in this world—do we not only see *him in the loudspeaker? No! We recognize every detail—how a lock of hair falls across his brow, how his hands mould and shape each word, how his hands clasp into a ring, indissoluble, when he speaks of the companionship and the unity of the Reich; we see his expression of contempt when he talks of the enemy, his shining eyes when he adds up the balance of victory in sober figures—all this we see in the loudspeaker. And when he then closes, with his moving words, and the Songs of our*

Nation sound, how reverently do we sing with them each time! And when the Berlin Sportpalast or the Kroll Opera House shakes with enthusiasm, how gladly we would call with them, 'Heil', and 'Heil' again, and once more, 'Heil'!

[In January 1943 Prüller left Vienna—more or less fit again—and was stationed in Moravia. In February, he left for Russia again. This part of the Diary is rather similar (though far less graphic, for Prüller was obviously tiring of writing down all his battle experiences) to the previous Russian section and has been entirely omitted here. In April, he was recommended as a candidate for a commission. In May, he was chosen by the Regiment to go to Katyn, where the Russians had murdered many Polish officers; Katyn provided the Nazis with a bit of welcome propaganda, and Prüller seems to have been genuinely shocked and disgusted by what he saw. On 26th May he learned that he had been promoted to *Fahnenjunker*, i.e. aspirant officer, 'the final step before becoming a *Leutnant*,' writes Prüller. In June he was sent home, first for a three-week leave, then to Officers' Candidate School in Moravia, and from there to the Officers' Training Camp in Königsbruck, near Dresden, where he arrived in August. At the beginning of December he finished the course successfully. He was sent back to Moravia, where in February his C.O. read the announcement that Prüller was now a *Leutnant*, retroactively effective as from 1st December 1943. It was certainly the high-point of his whole life. The following extract from the Diary was written at Officers' Training Camp, and though not strictly written in Russia, we have included it here, as the final part of the Russian Section.]

[Extracts from the Russian Diary of 1943]

September 1943

Thoughts about our Battle

The period from 30th January 1933 to 1st September 1939 compels a comparison with the period from 18th January 1871 to 1st August 1914. After the establishment of the Third Reich there followed—just as had been the case after the establishment of the Second Reich—an extraordinary flowering of activities in every conceivable field. Germany was rich, and its potentialities seemed endless. At the end of the nineteenth and beginning of the twentieth centuries—and equally so after the National Socialist revolution—this was a thorn in the flesh of our old enemies. Between these two periods there is one enormous difference, however: in the political leadership of the Reich. In the earlier period, bunglers pursued an unstable political line, whereas National Socialism has exchanged all that for political realism.

Then, as now, the enemy pretended not to have anything against the German peoples as such; then, they wanted to free us from our imperial monarchy and give us honour, work and culture; to provide us with a government which should flourish under the best sort of statesmanship. And they brought us a mutilation of our territories, the loss of our civil rights, seven million unemployed and as many part-time workers; they brought us nigger songs and ugly terracotta statues and about forty political parties.

It was the salvation of the Reich that a man arose from its lap [Prüller's metaphor] and with great effort—man for man, worker and intellectual, employee and artist—led the people to find itself again, and provided it with the one *Weltanschauung* which could unite the people. In truth, he re-established honour and prosperity in the Reich; the millions of unemployed were incorporated into the stream of industry and national economy; and a political leadership was established which may be described as ideal: and really one which grew out of the people themselves. And now these same enemies wish to free us from 'Nazism', to give us honour, work and culture. . . . It's the same old story.

If the opposing side had had the strength and courage to declare war earlier, they could perhaps have used as an excuse the rehabilitation of the army in 1935, the occupation of the Rhineland in 1936, the return of the *Ostmark* [Austria] in 1938, or the establishment of the Protectorate [of Bohemia and Moravia] in 1939. But they were not yet ready; the ring round the

Reich was not yet forged. Powerless, they had to watch how the Führer in a brilliant strategic coup prevented, for the time being, the war on two fronts.

Thus the war of plutocracy against National Socialism began. The German Wehrmacht's attacks against this enemy were terrible, in part ruinous. Even during the first phase of the war, Russia's friendship and neutrality proved to be no more than pretended. The Soviet plan was, after the enemies of the Reich had weakened it sufficiently, to attack Europe and, as its final goal, to achieve the world revolution. This revolution would have included the whole continent and doubtless, too, the British Isles and thus the whole earth. The Reich's attack thus prevented Europe and the rest of the world from becoming Bolshevik.

England: The peaceful competition for the world market, in which Germany threatened to become the dominant figure; the continual growth of the Reich's population and the concomitant necessity for more territory (return of our former colonies); England's obstinacy in retaining its old ideologies; the adherence to the execrable Treaty of Versailles, which divided the world into Haves and Have-Nots; and England's notorious fear of losing its predominant position in Europe through a united and mighty Germany—all these factors led to Germany's being hunted down. For 100 out of the last 240 years England has been waging wars for this and other reasons. There isn't a country on earth which hasn't suffered from a war with England.

Each one too weak by itself to bring the Reich to its knees, we cannot be surprised that Plutocracy and Bolshevism have joined together (and one must remember that the present British Prime Minister once openly declared Bolshevism to be the most dangerous curse of mankind)—after all, they are both run by the Jews. England is without conscience in betraying Europe and Western Civilization, and now its own peoples must fight for survival or the collapse of the Empire; it is without conscience in selecting, and if necessary betraying, its allies; without conscience in the manner in which it wages war; it is an insult to humanity. But we couldn't expect anything else from her.

Bolshevism: From the very beginning of the National Socialist revolution it was quite clear that peaceful coexistence between two such colossal empires as Germany and the Soviet Union, with their totally differing *Weltanschauungen*, could not continue to exist. National Socialism restored to the German peoples their honour; art and science could flourish unhindered; personal values were once more held in reverence; the peoples' freedom was all-important. Bolshevism has robbed the peoples of their self-respect, their personal freedom. By turning them into collective *Einheitsmenschen* they have made their peoples characterless cogs in what appears to be, organically speaking, a grandiose machine, but is spiritually a boundless waste.

The goal of Bolshevism was, and is, not to restrict its gospel of truth to Russia but to spread it throughout Europe and the whole world. The political doctrine of Bolshevism in no way represents a scientific theory; it is but a purely political act of world Jewry. And just as the Talmud teaches nothing except murder and destruction, so Bolshevism knows but one science: murder and destruction, cruel and barbaric murder, swift and certain destruction. Let us remember merely the murder of the Munich hostages in 1919, the terror houses of Kiev and Odessa, the murder of Czarist officers at Sevastopol, the government of Bela Kuhn in Hungary, the Civil War in Spain and, most recently, Katyn and Vinnitsa.

To root out the intelligentsia, to rob one of every personal possession, and finally the collectivization of every basic facet of life and thought—this is the least we can expect from a Bolshevik victory.

If we are not capable of toppling this Bolshevik colossus, the whole world's civilization will sink, just as in years past Rome and Athens broke under the storm of freed African and Syrian slaves. This storm of the underworld, let loose by the Jews, is fully as menacing as that which broke over the ancient world; but the dangers to which our twentieth-century civilization may be subjected by these barbaric Bolshevik beasts are far more terrifying than those of ancient times.

History has shown that Germany did not wish this war. The numberless offers of peace that the Führer made—even during the war and after gigantic victories—were described as 'concessions of the weak' and 'war fatigue'. Once the stone started to roll, it couldn't be stopped. It is clear that the path is difficult and that many more will fall by the wayside. But who, centuries later, will ask how many lives this global war cost? The primary factor will have been: they saved the integrity of the Reich . . .; or: they frivolously gave up the Reich.

Yes, it is no longer a fight of the Reich against its old enemies, no longer a flight between countries and territories, but a war of *Weltanschauungen*, a war of truth against untruth, a war between the Teutons [*Germanen*] and the Jews. Thus, the Teutons of this, the most respected continent on earth, are engaged in a war to the death with Plutocracy, allied with the murderers of the East. And it is Germany who must bear most of the brunt of this world-wide battle, and it is Germany who must shape the future history of the earth's peoples. Our goal is thus clear: famine or prosperity; destruction or construction; the end or the beginning; death or life! Verily it shall not be difficult for us to pursue this path!

4. THE FINAL PHASE: EXTRACTS FROM THE DIARY AND LETTERS OF 1944 AND 1945

[The last volume of Prüller's Diary was lost in the end-of-the-war confusion; we have included his reconstruction of it, made immediately afterwards, at the end. The turbulent events of the last year and a half of Prüller's military life have been preserved in a long series of letters to his wife, who kindly allowed us to copy them and to use extracts to fill in the last part of the Diary.

Prüller, now *Leutnant* in the German Wehrmacht, was again posted to Russia. On 24th February 1944 he arrived in Krakow, where several hundred officers collected, preparatory to being assigned to the Führer-Reserve of the South Ukranian Group of Armies. At this time Prüller's letters are full of advice on when and where to evacuate his wife, Henny, and the children.]

Krakow, 27th February 1944

Tomorrow morning we leave for Odessa and the Führer-Reserve of *Heeresgruppe* (Army Group) A. . . . Please do everything you can to get out of Vienna as quickly as possible. It would be a big relief for me to know that you and the children are in safety. They [the allied bombers] are certain to come. I hope you got over the first few hours after the parting. You know I would much rather see you when you look hard reality squarely in the face. Our duty requires a lot from both of us. . . .

En route to the East, 28th February 1944

. . . Yesterday a sentry in Krakow presented arms to me the first time. In fact they don't do that in wartime, only in foreign countries. Makes a good impression. Naturally they do it only to officers. Since it's the custom that an officer who is thus saluted for the first time gives the sentry something, I saw he was given 5 Mark. He must have boggled! I'm sure I was the only one who remembered.

En route to the East, 2nd March 1944

A few hours ago we crossed the German-Roumanian border. And at once the old, familiar picture returned: male and female creatures, crude and unappetizing, try to trade eggs, bacon, schnaps, tobacco. I'm saving all that for Odessa. . . . If only you and the children were out of Vienna by now. If you can help it, don't leave anything in the flat, particularly little things. The bigger the piece, the better.

Odessa, 7th March 1944

. . . The city looks like every other one in Russia: dirt, dirt, dirt. The Roumanian civil authorities don't seem to have accomplished much. As far as prices go, you would think we were heading for inflation. . . .

To return to the trip, when you are cooped up for a week in such close quarters, you get to know what people are really like. What went on—immaturity, unsoldierliness—is quite indescribable. . . . I won't describe it to you in any more detail; I'd rather tell you myself. But I know what your feelings are about discipline, whether soldier or civilian, whether abroad or at home, and I know how much you value honour and morals. And in view of what I saw, I can only assure you once again, my dear, that I shall not disappoint you. In any way. Neither in my conduct in general nor in matters which concern only us two. . . .

I've nothing of the classics to read any more and I should like something. I am thinking of *Faust*, something by Grillparzer or Schiller, or a Wagner libretto. . . .

I don't know if you've ever heard about the Odessa Opera, but it's one of the most famous abroad. Tickets are very difficult for us to obtain here, so I went to the Opera House and had myself announced to the Director. I introduced myself as 'Vienna Opera' and he nearly died of respect; I let him invite me, the day after tomorrow to *Traviata* and on Saturday to *Faust*. To smell the air of the theatre, the back stage noises, the bustle. . . . Oh, Henny, you don't know what it means to me! I don't think I can ever get away from it. I really must do something about it. Perhaps I can wangle [a position in] the Theater an der Wien after the war. . . . Plans for the future occupy my thoughts as always, and it's so nice to plan. . . . If only everything comes to a good end, Henny, look forward to such a lovely time. . . .

Odessa, 11th March 1944

. . . A watch here costs 1,500 to 2,500 Mark. Just out of curiosity I went into a shop and offered him my watch. He wanted to give me 600 Mark, but I'm sure I could have got him to give 800. . . . I have an idea: why not sell my second watch, the one at home? . . . If you ever send me a honey cake, cut out a piece from the bottom and put the watch inside, but seal it up again, otherwise the Feldpost people will find it. . . . My boots would be worth a fortune here, so don't let them go for a bagatelle; only for food (half a pig) or as much money. . . .

Odessa, 22nd March 1944

I just wrote to send out feelers about the Theater an der Wien: whom one should know, when one should begin. You can't start operations soon enough. . . . Do you know what I want to do when there's time? Go on with my French. 'Those with knowledge are masters, those without it slaves.' And I want you to go on with your English. We want to be perfect in everything we do.

31st March 1944 [*En route*]

. . . As far as the situation in the East is concerned, those of you at home can relax. Everything is proceeding *as planned.* In a short time you will see proof of it. . . .

Buzau, 15th April 1944

. . . I rather have the feeling that our letters, recently at least, are not what they were years ago. But you know, my Dearest, that I love you as much as ever. . . . Ah, if only those special words would flow, on paper, as they used to. . . . The moon, the stars, the sun, nature—they beckon to youth and love and Belonging-to-someone and Being-true-to-someone; and the heart grows wide, and one's thoughts circle in such a curious fashion round something and one would like to open one's arms and embrace, and, and . . . all that one has to push down inside oneself. One doesn't even have time, in peace and stillness, to think of the larger matters. Oh, Henny, what sacrifices we've had to make! And what still remains to be sacrificed at the Altar of the Future. Is it enough to know that the children will have better lives, one day? It *must* suffice. . . .

18th April 1944

. . . We left Buzau on Sunday, and via Barlad I arrived in Husi today. . . . It's a difficult route. With the railway you don't get anywhere, and the roads are quite beneath description. It's quite usual for trains to be a day late. If someone in Roumania says 'right away', you have to allow an hour; if he says 'in an hour', it's usually five. I cannot avoid thinking that the Roumanians—at least unwittingly—are sabotaging us. Terrible people. . . .

21st April 1944

Yesterday morning I arrived at my Battalion and was assigned to be Ordnance Officer of the 1st Regiment. . . . We're in the neighbourhood of Orheiu; it's quiet at the moment, apart from small fights. In the past few days, though, all hell was loose. . . .

24th April 1944

. . . The food here is excellent, and we drink wine instead of water. A wonderful place for wine! But the Balkans are so lazy, it stinks to Heaven. Put Germans here and you'd have Paradise. You can be sure, by the way, that the wine doesn't cause me to fall out of line. I know you think this is specially important. . . .

28th April 1944

. . . As to your last letters, dear 'Mutti' [nickname for mother], at first I nearly fell flat: we're to have another child. I reacted as you did: the news did not exactly cause me to jump for joy. Obviously. But if you consider the matter, things look different. And now I'm genuinely pleased. Listen, Mutti, perhaps it will be a boy—brown eyes, black hair, wouldn't that be something? My dear, I know there are many if's and but's; however: you can't cheat nature. . . . Both of us don't want to fritter away our lives in playful hours and nights. We always wanted to be examples, to lead the way. . . . I know it will be frightfully hard for you, but I also know that you will be brave and fight the good fight joyfully and successfully. . . . In my greetings and hopes for you, I include our new acquisition, too!

6th May 1944

. . . I own the translation of the Diary of a Russian officer, who fell in April. . . . I don't want to quote all the things it contains—better when I see you. [Prüller kept a copy of the diary in question, which is, apart from being very racy, a most interesting and revealing document.]

21st May 1944

. . . We are to be pulled out and sent to France. Naturally via Vienna. . . .

[Near Nîmes,] 9th June 1944

. . . We're quartered in a secluded castle, the quarters quite splendid: what rooms! what comfort! a marvellous library, games; it's simply terrific. . . .

What do you think about the invasion? I hope the affair will be cleaned up in a few weeks; it's unthinkable what it would be like to have to fight on the third front. . . . The population is very friendly, officers and N.C.O.s especially are highly regarded. I get along very well with my French; in a month I expect to speak perfectly again. I've already found a dictionary, but I don't want to take it, for it belongs to the castle library and the owner isn't here but in Paris. . . .

16th June 1944

. . . Once I did get to Nîmes and got rid of all my money. Four hundred Marks or 8,000 francs. But Mutti, the most beautiful things, all for you. Really! Actually I wanted to keep them for you till Christmas, but I can't carry them with me: they could get lost too easily. From today all leaves cancelled—in war theatres and at home, too. Führer's orders. To judge from today's Wehrmacht news bulletin, the revenge [*Vergeltung*] must have begun by now. . . .

2nd July 1944

Recently I had a special assignment which took me along the Mediterranean to the Spanish border, then into the Pyrenees and a few hundred metres into Spanish territory. Mutti, it was a fantastic drive. The ocean blue as ink. . . . Henny, after our victory, our honeymoon will take us to Holland and France. We'll get hold of a car, we will be able to get them cheaply from the Wehrmacht; then you take your driver's test and off we go. . . .

21st July 1944

When they told me today of the attempt on the Führer's life, I was speechless. Imagine, my good Henny, if this indescribable crime had succeeded and these swindlers of our people had pulled off their deed! The result would have been utter chaos. For nothing would have been five years of fighting and pain and work and sacrifice, for nothing the lives laid down by millions of Kameraden. Bolshevism would have been the only winner, the front would have melted away, the country [Germany] a bed of ruins.

That Providence spared the Führer is in itself a sign that we are on the right path. . . . A bloody broom—it can't be too bloody—must put things right! . . . The first time in German history that such a thing was done by officers. It's a revolting scandal! No Austrian officer was among them—I should think *not*. Reorganization of the Wehrmacht, that would seem to be Himmler's job now. . . . My dearest Henny! Now it's all or nothing! Fight to the very end. Victory or death. Our motto: everything for our dear fatherland, everything for the Führer!

[On 25th July, Prüller was attacked by partisans and severely wounded; lying in a pool of blood, he managed to reach into his pocket and pull out his notebook—pierced by a bullet hole—and start to write 'Ich bin verwu . . .' (I am wound . . .) before he fainted. This notebook, spattered in dried blood, still exists.]

27th July 1944 [*written in another hand:*]

My condition does not allow me to report to you what happened. But I know that you will receive this news with your usual steadfastness: on the 25th I was wounded in a terror attack. I'm lying in Nîmes, well taken care of. . . . I intend to get someone to accompany me and then to go straight to the reserve hospital in Zwettl [Lower Austria]. . . .

Valence, 2nd August 1944

[Prüller could not travel yet, and was sent to Valence to recover.]

It [the wound] will take a long time to heal, although it's not quite as bad as it looks: shot in the neck, right; hole in my chest the size of an egg, collar bone broken on the right, one or two ribs a bit under the weather, tip of the lung punctured, upper and lower part of the arm, thumb and first finger dead because nerve damaged. Sounds terrible, but it's not. . . . It happened this way: I was in my car, examining roads. In St. Hyppolite—50 kilometres north-west of Nîmes—Mayerhofer, Lipska and I, peacefully sitting in a hotel garden, were attacked by 20 terrorists. I nearly bled to death, and the terrorists wanted to finish me off; but they thought I'd had it anyway. Five hours later I was in the operating room. . . .

Valence, 9th August 1944

It really doesn't look very rosy anywhere you turn: Henny, I'm a born optimist, but how shall this end? A world full of enemies, all round us they set out for the death-blow, with an enormous superiority of men and material, weapons and munition and machines; one success after another for them. And we? . . .

Valence, 12th August 1944

. . . Do you remember that you once sent me some words by Knut Hamsun which (naturally) I carry in my pocket-book: 'Fragt jemand was die Liebe ist, so ist sie nichts als ein Wind, der in den Rosen rauscht und wieder dahin stirbt. Oft aber ist sie auch wie ein unverbrüchliches Siegel, das das ganze Leben lang dauert, bis zum Tode.'[1] I just read the book from which

[1] If someone asks, what is love? it is nothing but the wind, that whispers in the roses and dies out again. But often it is like an unbreakable bond, which lasts one's whole life, even unto death.

it comes. Fantastic! Nowadays I mostly read *Mein Kampf*. That does one good in these difficult times; it's the easiest way for one to keep faith. I recommend it to everyone.

In the nights I often wonder how it is that I'm still here and not under a simple wooden cross. We're to be allowed to enjoy our lives and our love yet! As I was lying on the ground and writing in my notebook a last greeting to you [*vide supra*] with my left hand, I had to give up after a few words—so weak was I then. And then I remembered how it was in July, when I went home for those few hours, and the children rushed up to me and said: 'Daddy's come home!' It is not a question of me personally any longer. Of course I enjoy living; but I've made a reckoning with myself for some time, and if a real soldier's death comes to me, and I die with an order on my lips, or even a smile, that's all right with me. But I want to help the children with their first steps in life, and to realize my plans with them; I wanted to thank you once more, even if only one word, for your love and faithfulness, for your belief in me; and then the French woman returned with the doctor, gave me a swallow of water, raised my head and whispered to me in French: it will be all right. And I answered her: 'il faut', it must. And then everything happened as it had to happen. And yesterday and today and tomorrow—every day—my thoughts are always with you and the children. . . .

[*Alexandersbad*,] *10th September 1944*

You know my ever-present optimism; it's there now as it always was. I am sure everything will take a turn for the better. It can't be that a people to whom the world obviously owes everything could disintegrate. There's no nation more energetic, more faithful, more courageous, more efficient. Our accursed enemies will not conquer us, even if now the bitter struggle for our beloved fatherland seems quite hopeless. . . . It is quite unthinkable that everything should have been for nothing. . . .

[Meanwhile Prüller managed to get sent to Vienna. Henny and the children had found a quiet village in the country where they were living.]

Vienna, 24th September 1944

We arrived safely and punctually yesterday. . . . *En route* I was able to see some of the damaged houses . . . Alserstrasse from the Gürtel to the Hausindustrie, Kinderspitalgasse and the region near the Brunnenmarkt, as well as the Neulerchenfelderstrasse have been badly hit. They are working hard to clear away the rubble. . . .

Vienna, 17th November 1944

. . . Last time I wrote what I thought of V-2: a tremendous gain, at any rate, over V-1. . . . I consider it possible that we may develop the splitting of the atom to such an extent that it can be harnessed for war service. . . .

[Prüller managed to see his wife before he was sent to a recovery hospital near Dresden, where he arrived on 11th January 1945.]

[*Near Dresden,*] *16th January 1945*

. . . I have been suggested as a candidate for the National Socialist *Führungsoffiziere* school. These are officers at division and regiment level, who are to support the battle from the philosophical [*weltanschaulicher*] standpoint and to educate the troops along these lines. The Nazi *Führungsoffizier* is not, however, to be compared in any way to the Russian *Kommissar*. The entertainments officer here thinks I am just cut out for the job. I should be pleased if it worked out.

Please send me, registered, all my political papers which I left at home: SS membership card, refugee card [for the time that Prüller left Austria, before the *Anschluss*, and lived in Germany], my party membership card. I don't remember a single date or number and I shall need them for the NSFO [*Naz. Soz. Führungsoffizier*] school. . . . As far as my SS uniform goes, I entirely agree that you give it away for the general good, because I know what it means for a soldier to freeze. I only don't want to give it to a collection depot, but to my SS *Sturm* for an SS man who joins the *Volkssturm*, or rather for a top-ranking member of the SS who has been detailed for *Volkssturm* duty. I am sure you think as I do.

[*Near Dresden*,] *19th January 1945*

. . . Yesterday Hans Fritzsche [chief news commentator of the German Radio] spoke to us. It was interesting mainly because we could meet him personally: winning, good-looking, ironic corner of the mouth, about 45 years of age; but he couldn't tell us anything new. He said it was important for us to remain a power when Plutocracy and Bolshevism got in each other's hair. A very vague hope, that, and I don't believe it will work on *in this war*. The east is marching again and has won a lot of ground. . . . They are already 120 kilometres from Mährisch-Ostrau. Henny, we mustn't give up hope; I still hope that spring or summer will bring a change of course. Nevertheless they aren't sure whether the 'Herr' [old Junker guard] should be abolished or not! As if we hadn't other problems. Or whether the period from *Leutnant* to *Oberleutnant* should be raised from three to 3½ years!

Vienna, 26th January 1945

. . . The situation is at present very depressing, and it looks as if all our enormous sacrifices were for nothing; as if our 25 years of struggle were for nothing and thus that it was all a big lie. But it isn't that far yet. They triumph too soon, our accursed enemies, and we'll tip the scales at the last minute. Hennerl, if you could have seen all the misery that the poor Upper Silesians and the Breslauers had to go through, you could only weep for pity.

Breslau had to be evacuated within *one hour*; the last trains out of Gleiwitz left under fire from enemy artillery within the city itself; hundreds died *en route*—froze to death—and most of them couldn't take more than a handbag, a child on each arm, and no goal, no hope to see a warm room. . . . What went on in Dresden, in Prague, and all along the whole way to Vienna is the greatest German tragedy. . . . And when you get to Vienna afterwards, you can only be ashamed that the much vaunted 'golden Vienna heart' has turned into a nasty, egocentric and selfish thing. The way the population behaves to these poorest of the poor [refugees] is simply scandalous. They threw out of the tram a woman from the Sudetenland with the words: 'first the Viennese, then the Bohemians'! [in Viennese dialect even nastier]. . . . I leave tomorrow for Dresden. . . .

[*Dresden,*] *1st February 1945*

The trip was a horrible mess; no trains run on schedule any more. The stream of refugees increases continually (rather than decreasing) and I kept thinking of you and the children and praying that that wouldn't happen to you. . . . The situation has worsened considerably. Something must happen soon, or else. . . . Despite my optimism, I have already worked out the situation that can happen: there are only two possibilities—either Russian occupation or an autonomous Austria. Quite unthinkable, for both would be all too dreadful. . . .

[Meanwhile Prüller was, as he wished, sent to NSFO school near Bamberg, where he arrived on the night of 9th February 1945.]

[*Near Bamberg,*] *9th February 1945*

. . . Here nothing is happening—long blocks of barracks, here and there a man from the organization. It will take a while till things get organized. [11th February 1945:] . . . The rooms for the *Fahnenjunker* [aspirant officers, in this case aspirant NSFO officers] are not even ready yet, and there's no heat yet (steam heating)—no Kissem, no writers, no personnel at all, in a word, abso-bloody-lutely the way it ought not to be. And to top the cake, the *Fahnenjunker* are trapesing in all the time since yesterday. You can imagine that they nearly chewed the carpet several times.

When you see something like that, you can only quote the words of one of my friends who said, a year ago: 'The Germans are intelligent: everything is over-organized.' Most of the teachers are old school-pigs, so it will be difficult for me to keep my nose above water. First question: had I already attended a special school? No, but five years at the front. All very well, that doesn't count here, we have other guiding principles, is what he said. . . . Bamberg is a pretty little town with many old buildings. A wonderful, forgotten corner which I had noticed in 1939 when I was here, I found again, right on the first day. . . . The situation has again worsened in the past few days: the Russians have won more ground in the direction of Dresden. But as I said before, we've not yet played our last card; in a few weeks there will *have* to be a change, or else—that's clear to the gentlemen here, too.

[*Near Bamberg,*] *15th February 1945*

I have the impression that a general air offensive has been started, at the end of which they intend to wring out of us a capitulation. It's just crazy what's happening here in the whole Reich, and in the west they've now begun—quite unsystematically—to flatten out every little parish-pump village with their bombs. They want to make an end of things at any price. But we aren't nearly as finished as they believe. . . .

[*Near Bamberg,*] *19th February 1945*

. . . You know I don't think much of political lectures, because nothing much of any use comes from them. But today an *Unteroffizier* from the Personnel Section—he's an SA *Sturmführer* from East Prussia—spoke to us on the theme: 'Who shall win? Horst Wessel or Judah?' Thoroughly excellent in content, structure and execution. Later we're to have other VIPs, but who knows. . . .

[*Near Bamberg,*] *22nd February 1945*

. . . We have air raid alarm four times a day. After midnight, in the morning, afternoon, and evening. Alarm just sounded this minute, the fifth we've had today. In the morning there was quite a raid over B[amberg] and the damage is not to be sniffed at. Even the old part of the city, near the Cathedral, got it. . . .

[*Near Bamberg,*] *11th March 1945*

Your fears about the present precarious situation are only too easily understood, especially as it's very bad in the west and almost the whole part on the other side of the Rhine has been given up for lost. But that's no reason to hang your head so low, to get so desperate, and to want to throw in the sponge. It will all change, and soon, too. I'm sure they'll fold up like a saggy tent when we attack again. They've never been able to hold out in such cases. . . . Nevertheless, or rather because of our difficulties, we must continue to believe in the general German victory, because there's nothing else except to win or to die. What has happened in those parts occupied by the Soviets gives us an excellent preview of what will happen to the whole population if we (for instance) give up the Balkans.

Anyway, we're still very lucky. Look, dear Henny, at all those people who don't know where their families are; women who don't know if their husbands are still fighting, or perhaps already dead; soldiers whose wives, children and parents have fled somewhere from the Russians or are booty in the hands of those loathsome animals. They don't know anything of each other's fate, and yet they've not given up their faith in the Reich, its people, its victory. Here in the school there are many of them, teachers and *Junker*. And they must bite their tongues, and stick it out and go on doing their duty. It's that way, isn't it, Henny, and we don't want to yap at all the difficulties (which are many); we must go on saying: others have it far, far worse. That way we'll get over this period. . . .

[*Near Bamberg,*] *20th March 1945*

You are quite right when you surmise that the ground is

burning under my feet because I'm just an onlooker. I can't help it. For me these concepts of Fatherland, faith in the thing I'm doing, in the Führer, my readiness to jump into the fray, are not just empty words: and I'm ready at any time to turn my belief into action. It's true that I can't lead my troops into battle, and who knows if I can ever manage such a thing again physically; but there are many other things to be done.

[Earlier Prüller, after his last bout in the hospital, had considered 'joining Dr. Goebbels's sphere'.]

Slowly I've got used to the fact that—at least for a very long time to come—I'll have to say good-bye to the front; but every piece of news from out there, whether by letter or by word of mouth, makes me want to start all over again. And like lightning in a clear sky I received a letter from Hagmüller. He informs me hastily that the General of the NSFO would like to have me with the Division, and I should let him know by the quickest route if I am physically capable of accepting. The Division NSFO hasn't anything to do with the battlefront, of course; it's a staff set-up, though not one to sell to a life insurance company. But where can you find a safe place nowadays anyway? A wonderful task: to orient 20,000 men politically, to lead them politically that is; to activate all their spiritual, moral force, to raise it to the highest power, and thus to influence the attacking spirit of a whole division!

You've known me all these years now, and you will guess right away what I did. I accepted with the greatest of alacrity. . . . I wrote today and sent a message via the teletape, too, that I am physically capable of doing the NSFO and request a job with general headquarters of the armoured troops. Unfortunately our teletape in Bamberg has collapsed, also that at Nürnberg, but perhaps it will get through to them in the next few days. . . . We might have a fortnight's leave beforehand, in beautiful weather; wouldn't that be wonderful? . . . Don't be sad at what I've done, Henny; but rather proud that I'm not one of those who works every possible angle to remain behind the lines. . . . Think of the Führer's words which he once said to his *Gauleiter*: 'If only 10 per cent of the German population were true idealists, the war would have been won long ago.' I wish to belong to those happy few. And you should belong, too. . . .

[*Near Bamberg,*] *26th March 1945*

Only a quick note to let you know that tremendous things have happened. Probably you've heard it on the wireless. The Anglo-American troops have broken out of Oppenheim and pushed through to Aschaffenburg, 130 kilometres from here, moreover they have landed airborne troops near Fulda, 100 kilometres from here. . . . In great haste they [the Germans] are organizing a new army in Bamberg, and because of this the school will probably be dissolved. . . . The situation is again very serious, but we must continue to hold our heads high in this decisive moment. We've got to stop them. . . . It can't go on like this; there must be a change. And this change will come, I'm sure of it.

[Pruller's final War Diary, as he reconstructed it shortly before the cessation of hostilities.]

This, the fourteenth MS. volume of my War Diary, was lost together with my baggage. I am unable to set down the precise details therein recorded, and can only reconstruct the events, but I believe that I have not omitted anything important.

Prüller, Lieutenant

April 1945

It is sad how few Germans still talk of a decisive change in our fight for life and death; how few still use the word 'victory': and in the autumn of 1942 the whole population at home, and of course we soldiers, were more than convinced of a great German victory. At that time 150,000,000 in the Reich yelled their throats hoarse over our incomparable victories; whereas today it is only the idealists of the Nazi pre-war *Kampfzeit* [time of fighting] who, in tight-lipped aggression, hold on to their beliefs and are not confounded in their loyalty to the Führer;

not even when the earth threatens to crash over our heads at any moment.

It is true that the defeats are crushing, and a glance at the map of Europe and the Greater German Reich suggests even to an amateur that there is no way out of this sad impasse. But that is the shameful thing about the majority of the German people: we are all too easily swayed, too easily enthusiastic, too intoxicated, when we are doing well; but we threaten to give ourselves up when the going is not so good; we're born attackers but bad defenders, especially in that we are much too much concerned with ourselves and our own, small, personal possessions. A woman in the village Kemmern, 10 kilometres north of Bamberg, wanted to stick a manure fork into me because I, with a few soldiers, held up the advancing Americans a few hours, because during this time her house was hit by enemy tank shells; or the inhabitants of Breitengussbach, who hoisted white flags behind the backs of my soldiers—small in numbers and badly armed—who were holding off an overwhelming majority for half a day (!);[1] or the Volkssturm, who in numerous places actually opened the tank barriers to the enemy—all these are convincing signs of the conduct of the German people in this period of deepest misery. German people! With wounded heart I must ask you: how could you have so changed your minds? Your soldiers, their bodies covered with blood and exhausted as if before the last sleep, attempt with their very hands to hold back the enemy's vast superiority in material and numbers; the reports of what happened in ancient history are nothing compared to the thousands of deeds which our men accomplish every day. And you, German people, throw yourselves unthinkingly into the arms of your merciless enemies, so that (for the moment) your houses shall be spared; but you throw away not only your lives but also your honour. Just a short time ago all of you were rejoicing in National Socialism; you never tired of crying 'Heil Hitler!' If it were not for those who thought otherwise—and, *ach*! there are so few—one would really have to ask: did you deserve anything but your ruin, O Germany?

[1] Prüller's exclamation mark.

Just look at the majority of your soldiers, at the head of whom is the dearly beloved Führer; how they still try to stop the flood; how in the ruins of the Reich's capital, surrounded on all sides, they fight an unparallcled last battle! Old men became heroes, children became titans, women and girls even take on man's bloody job in this merciless war. Can you not, German people, take this one example as a guide to your conduct in this heroic battle? Have you not been shown, in the defence of Breslau, in the conduct of civilians, Hitler Jugend, party members, Volkssturm, SS, Wehrmacht, that even in the hopeless situation one can remain steadfast?

Verily, I know what you think when a Göring leaves his post at a moment like this; but I know you must be listening to enemy broadcasts, because the number of our own radio stations has so diminished; I know that the Western and Italian fronts have more or less collapsed, that we have lost more than half our territory [*Gaue*], that in Munich there are criminals who wish to play at being heroes, that a general is said to have released all soldiers and officers from their oath of loyalty to the Führer; but because of such things should we lay down our arms, and so easily surrender Fatherland, future, occupation, family—yes, even our own lives? Yes, for our personal ruin would be the result of such action—not only the end of this wonderful Reich. Germany divided by two enemies; and because it cannot be avoided, they will become enemies of each other, and the battlefield will be our land; drenched in blood, the rest of our villages and cities destroyed, our 2,000-year-old culture wiped out—that will be the harvest we reap from our present seeds of faithlessness.

Think of the millions of dead in far-flung theatres of war, who with glassy eyes and bloodless lips managed to stammer as their last word—full of inner peace and in deep idealism—the Führer's name or that of our everlasting fatherland; think of their dear ones, who made this incredible sacrifice for that man and this country. Think of our towns in ruins, of the many living war casualties, of the things we did without, the sorrows, the problems of nearly six years; think of these things and you cannot do otherwise but close your ears to the seductive words of our enemies.

Look: young divisions are already attacking, to come to the aid of the capital; in the south, the eastern front is now stable again; and there will come other fronts, and the course of the war will change. Until then you must remain firm, even if things appear to be hopeless. It cannot, must not, have been for naught; there must not be an end fashioned by the will of our enemies.

The future is in thy hands, O *Volk*.

POSTSCRIPT

The German soldier, Wilhelm Prüller, whose diary of World War II is printed here for the first time, was a Nazi: but not one of the bloodthirsty, dehumanized Nazi monsters, a diary of whose activities would make far more sensational, if no more tragic reading than that of the Viennese private who crossed the Polish-German frontier in September 1939 and became a small cog in the huge machinery of the Wehrmacht.

Prüller was a loving husband, a good family man; he served the Fatherland faithfully, unswervingly, courageously. He believed implicitly in the moral right of his side; he considered ultimate German victory certain and deserved, and avoided being killed without fearing Death. He possessed a genuine soldier's mind, with all the qualifications necessary to make him a useful and efficient part of the German war machine.

In short, Wilhelm Prüller suffered from that peculiar sort of brain fever which a good soldier must possess if he is not to become a coward and a deserter. The fact that he happened to be an Austrian serving the swastika is of secondary importance. If he had been born in Birmingham, Brooklyn or Novosibirsk, he would have been an equally good soldier—except that he would have worn an English, American or Russian uniform. If he had been born in England, he might not have kept a war diary—the reasons why the 'Dichter und Denker' Prüller kept one would in any case have been different from those which might have motivated Bill Priller, Sergeant in the Queen's Black Horse, to write such a diary—but if he had, we should have read joking or shocked references to the Wehrmacht or the S.S. monsters instead of political tirades against the capitalist brigand Churchill and the lice-ridden, stinking Russian villages.

POSTSCRIPT

In a sense, the *Diary of a German Soldier* is the reverse side of the world which produced the Diary of Anne Frank: and just as Anne Frank was an unknown (though articulate) member of the persecuted Jewish community in Amsterdam, so Wilhelm Prüller was an unknown (though articulate) member of the machine which forced Anne Frank into hiding and subsequently into the gas chamber. It would be, we feel, wrong for history to judge the Second World War entirely from the summit level: not that we in any way disparage the publication of memoirs by Montgomery, Churchill, Manstein, Dönitz, *et al.*, but there are obviously historical perspectives which are better seen through the reverse end of the telescope—through the sensitive eyes of a Jewish teenager and the not-so-sensitive but alert eyes of the conquering Wehrmacht private.

In October 1959, when Wilhelm Prüller, ex-Oberleutnant of the German Army, delivered to us the complete manuscript of his war diaries, he was no longer a soldier. There was no longer any more enemy territory to take or to hold; there was no longer a great cause for which one could die if not happily, at least in the serene assurance that it was for a good cause and for a certain victory. In 1959, Prüller ran a small shop in a dreary outer district of Vienna, selling rubber articles, souvenirs and Catholic 'Devotionalien'. He was thin, almost to emaciation, his once clean-cut, Teutonically handsome face lined and bloated from alcohol, his eyes bloodshot and heavy-lidded. But the old *Soldatengeist* lived on in him, grotesquely, incredibly: he was still true to his beliefs. On the fourth finger of his right hand hc wore a heavy ring with a large, flat black stone, from which shone dully the gold engraving of the SS runic sign. And as he sipped his cognac, it was clear that he still believed in it all, hopelessly but doggedly; believed, too, that what he had done was honourable and 'right'. Prüller's personal tragedy, measured against the tally of Auschwitz and Belsen, Dachau and Buchenwald, can hardly excite our sympathy; but judged not as a single person but as a typical (yes, even for Austria) specimen of the Nazi machine in which he functioned with such smooth precision, Prüller's diary reveals more forcefully (because more primitively) the appalling effectiveness of the German propaganda machine on its own nation and, apart from that, the efficiency with which the German Army could instil into a man of, one presumes, reasonable intelligence the fanaticism necessary for him to be the excellent soldier he obviously was. Apart from everything else, Prüller's diary is a grim lesson in how to make a first-rate fighter.

Prüller's background and the atmosphere in which he grew up—Austria in the 1920's and 1930's—were excellently suited to prepare him for his German fanaticism.

He was born in Vienna on 14th January 1916. It was the middle of World War I, the time when the blockade of the Allies began to take effect, when famine and poverty were spreading throughout Austria and Germany, even to protected villages far behind the lines. Prüller was not yet three years of age when the Central Powers collapsed and the ancient Hapsburg Monarchy was dissolved: an empire on which the sun had once never set disappeared in the chaos of 1918. The huge Austro-Hungarian Monarchy, which had encompassed a vast territory with some fifty million subjects, shrank overnight to a small country of seven million inhabitants; century-old economic ties were broken by the new borders, and the proud capital city of Vienna with its two million citizens, from which had streamed a culture over the whole of Central Europe, suddenly found itself the watermelon head of a state unwilling and, it appeared, unable to exist. The Emperor was forced to leave the country, though the aristocracy was allowed to remain and its land not confiscated.

The tiny new Republic of Austria had an unhappy and inauspicious birth. In the Parliament in Vienna were the representatives of the three principal political parties: the Christian Socialist, the Social Democrats and the *Grossdeutsche Partei*. The first two, despite all their deep-rooted differences, were agreed with the third on one point: Austria could not exist alone and must be attached to Germany—the main platform of the *Grossdeutsche Partei*, whose cry for 'Anschluss' brought about the very name of the party, 'Greater Germany'.

In one of the few measures to which all three parties at once agreed, it was decided to call the new state 'Deutsch Österreich', a curiously hopeful title which one can still find on old stamps of the period. The victorious Allies were, of course, able to prevent this *Anschluss* from becoming an accomplished fact: the Treaty of St. Germain forbade it; but scarcely anyone, in post-war Austria, thought that the new Republic could survive without the Reich.

In this confused political situation, Wilhelm Prüller grew up. His father was a type-setter, a member of the downtrodden, rebellious working classes. Prüller's father was not one of the rebels, however, but a good, quiet, conservative Catholic. He had to give up his profession as a result of lead poisoning, and became a day labourer for any firm with whom he could get work: first as a house painter in a glass factory, then as overseer for a building firm, finally as a stage-hand in the *Burgtheater*.

Money and food were tight at home. The son went to school (the *Volkschule*) in Hernals, a workers' district. Like the other children, he played soccer and handball in his free time. He was brought up in the Roman Catholic religion, and became a member of the *Christlich-Deutschen Turner*, a Catholic sport organization; he would have liked to join the *Pfadfinder*, too, that Boy-Scout organization which in Austria was even more severely Catholic than the *Turnverein* but with less accent on the 'Deutsch' and more on the international.

To trek through the deep green Austrian forests, following half-hidden paths through the lonely wooded mountains of Tyrol; to set up tents and camp in the open; to wear a uniform with a broad-brimmed hat and a cheerful kerchief; to carry a stick with tapered end in iron (almost as good as a real gun!)—here was the most harmless and (from the standpoint of modern psychology) 'safest' way to sublimate, without harming anyone or anything, the first traces of the 'soldier sickness' which, like mumps and measles, teenage boys generally contract. And to be a *Pfadfinder* was little Prüller's dearest wish.

But the money wasn't there for it: the uniform, the shirt, the hat, the iron-pointed stick and the kerchief—those cost more than the *quondam* type-setter could scrape together; and thus Prüller did not become a Boy Scout.

There was, however, another *Jugendorganisation*, whose members also sported uniforms, albeit consisting only of a brown shirt, black tie and white stockings. These shirts, ties and stockings cost nothing: wealthy 'patrons' were glad to pay for them. And like the Boy Scouts, this youth group marched, hiked through hill and dale, pitched their tents and sang lusty songs round the evening campfire (in the deep shadows of forests so green, so German). And everything was a bit more organized, more efficient, more military. This organization was called the *Hitler-Jugend.*

The *Hitler-Jugend* was, even then, the pre-military group designed to train its Ayrian members (not so blond in Austria, perhaps) for the private army of the N.S.D.A.P., the so-called SA (*Sturm-Abteilung*). At that time, the SA was not the only private 'party army' which existed in Austria; it was not even the strongest or most important. There was also the rather sinister *Heimwehr*, an ultra-conservative, strongly Catholic, half-Fascist *Bürgergarde*, patterned after Mussolini's blackshirts, supported and encouraged by the Catholic Church and the Christian Socialist Party. And finally, there was the *Schutzbund*, the highly military, uniformed shock troops of the Social Democrats. Austria was living on a powder keg, to which only a spark was needed to ignite a civil war. In 1927, one year before Prüller joined the *Hitler-Jugend*, an Austrian Court refused to condemn a party of right-wing terrorists who had killed several Social Democrats in a brutal attack; a furious, hysterical mob stormed the Palace of Justice in Vienna, set it on fire and slaughtered the police guarding it. The spectre of civil war grew steadily. The aristocracy—perhaps the most degenerate in Europe—listlessly supported the Christian Socialists, and the Catholic Church was inexorably bound up with that party; against them were the workers—the Social Democrats and Communists. The political chaos of 1918 had become, ten years later, solidified into a class war, as yet undeclared, but expected (indeed being prepared) by workers, politicians and the church alike. The Nazis capitalized on this hopeless situation by helping to create constant unrest and turmoil among the populace. Anti-semitism, long entrenched in the Austrian mentality, was fed by the incoming streams of penniless bearded Jewish beggars from Poland and Silesia where the poverty was even more grinding than in Vienna.

Prüller joined the *Hitler-Jugend* shortly before the Wall Street crash. The economic situation in Austria continued to worsen: there were soon half a million unemployed (nearly a tenth of the whole population). People starved on the streets, thousands of prostitutes and beggars swarmed over the once-proud Imperial City. Many survived the icy winters only by stealing coal from the railway yards; skilled workers became street musicians to keep their families alive.

In 1933, Hitler came to power in Germany, and in this year Prüller, now 17, left the *Hitler-Jugend* to join the S.S. (*Schutz-Staffel*) of the N.S.D.A.P. The so-called 'black SS' (because of the black uniforms they wore) were, contrary to the SA, or broad mass of Nazi storm troopers, originally intended to be the personal bodyguards of the Nazi leaders; the SS was divided into 'Standarten' of approximately regimental strength. One of the two Vienna 'house standards' was the SS-Standarte 89, and it was this group which Prüller joined.

Shortly afterwards, the Nazi party was banned in Austria, and with it the SA and SS Prüller remained in the N.S.D.A.P. all the same, quietly paying his dues to the now illegal organization. He worked as a salesman, at first in a Jewish textile store, later in a good-class shop.

Meanwhile the political situation in Austria had reached the point of no return. The Vienna City Government—Socialist pioneers in building huge blocks of flats for the workers—had constructed them also with an eye to using their heavy, ugly masses of concrete twistings and turnings as armed fortresses in case the Christian party should attack them. In the year 1934 took place one of the most shameful episodes in the history of post-war Europe, in which proud Vienna became the scene of a totally unfair fight between the workers and the government.

POSTSCRIPT

Twenty-five years later (and indeed even in the 1930's) what happened in Austria has been overshadowed by the events in Germany, in Ethiopia, in Spain, in the Rhineland, and, of course, by Austria itself four years later. Its present historical obscurity in no way reduces the grossness of the original crime.

On 5th March 1933 the Christian Socialist Government under Chancellor Engelbert Dollfuss used a parliamentary crisis to seize the entire governmental power for itself and, by circumventing the *Nationalrat* (Parliament), to destroy the last remnants of Austria's young and fragile democracy. The crisis revolved round a point of quite secondary importance (as so often when a democracy is about to topple), and in the squabble the three Presidents of the Nationalrat—a Christian Socialist, a Social Democrat and a *Grossdeutscher*—resigned simultaneously. Dollfuss acted swiftly: he declared that Parliament was incapable of normal procedure and therefore incompetent to pass resolutions; and his clever legal experts dug up a long-forgotten law, the *Kriegswirtschaftliches Ermächtigungsgesetz*, which the Emperor's government had, during World War I, created in order that special laws might in time of war be enacted without parliamentary approval. This 'emergency powers' law should have been revoked after the Kaiser and his Government collapsed, but in the post-war confusion it had been overlooked and was thus, technically speaking, still law.

In January 1934 the Dollfuss Government came under pressure from Italy and Jugoslavia, who wanted the Austrian Socialist Party liquidated. The Government thereupon began to confiscate Socialist papers, break up their meetings, and search workers' houses for weapons. It was during just such a 'house search' in Linz that the Austrian powder keg was ignited: it was February 1934, when workers and the Linz police exchanged shots.

The Social Democrats answered by calling on the workers to revolt. Members of the Social Democratic Party's private army, the *Schutzbund*, occupied the huge blocks of workers' flats, dug out rifles and machine-guns from hidden caches in cellars, often cemented into the walls in anticipation of such an event, and prepared for a siege; simultaneously they attempted to take over police stations, railway yards, and the like. A general strike was called. The Army, firmly on the side of the Government, and the *Heimwehr* (the Christian Socialists' private army) counter-attacked; they brought up light artillery and shot down the workers like rats. Whole floors of the concrete workers' houses were reduced to rubble, and the Socialists saw it was hopeless: they capitulated after a few days of the merciless cannon fire. Many Socialist leaders fled across the border (usually to Switzerland or Czechoslovakia), and those who remained were arrested. Drum-head courts-martial condemned many to instant death; in Wöllersdorf the Government erected the first *Konzentrationslager*, or concentration camp, on Austrian soil—only it was called *Anhaltelager*. Brutality on the scale of the later German concentration camps did not occur, of course; but the fact remains that almost all Social Democratic M.P.s disappeared behind the barbed wire.

That was the end of Austrian democracy. Dollfuss set up a dictatorship based on the Italian Fascist state, and this new 'Ständestaat' at once forbade opposition newspapers and set up a harsh, clerical-minded censorship of news, etc. Political freedom, except for the aristocracy, Catholic Church and such citizens as were known to be pro-Government, ceased to exist.

The illegal Nazis, and with them the SS-member, Wilhelm Prüller, were spectators rather than participants in this Austrian tragedy. The moment hostilities ended between the Socialists and the Government, however, the Nazis moved in, and a wave of terror swept the country. Bombs were hurled into Jewish shops and businesses; at night swastikas were painted on walls and churches; ancient ritual fires gleamed on lonely mountain peaks of Styria, Tyrol and Land Salzburg. The Nazi Government in Germany put increasing pressure on the weak Austrian clerical dictatorship. By means of the so-called 'Tausend-Mark-Sperre' (every German wishing to visit Austria was forced to pay a 'tax' of 1,000 Marks to the German Government), they made it virtually impossible for Germans to take their holidays in Austria, thus ruining Austrian tourism—a large source of the country's annual income even today. Austria's economic plight grew steadily more desperate.

Then, in July 1934, the Vienna-based SS-Standarte 89 struck. Camouflaged in Austrian Army uniforms, their Komandos—Prüller was not, as it happens, among them—occupied the Chancellor's Office in the Ballhausplatz and the Austrian State Radio, 'RAVAG'. Dollfuss was shot and bled to death before help could be summoned. Only Mussolini's threat to move his troops, stationed on the Brenner Pass, into Austria prevented Hitler from ordering the Wehrmacht to occupy the country.

Once again the Austrian Government was able to put down the revolt. Kurt von Schuschnigg took over Dollfuss's post; the murderers were hanged; but by this time, it was too late to stop events. Mussolini, hitherto Austria's only protector against German imperialism, attacked Ethiopia and gradually lost the traditional goodwill of the Western Powers. He needed Hitler's friendship: Hitler's price was Austria, and Mussolini agreed.

After having eked out a miserable existence for several years (as salesman, secretary to the chief of the claque in the 'Volksoper', etc.), Prüller decided, in 1937, to emigrate to Germany. Aged 21, he arrived in Munich and reported to the 'Austrian Legion'; as a member of the SS, he was sent to the SS-*Sammellager* (or Collecting Point) in Thüringen, where he awaited the Anschluss with Austria.

He had not long to wait. The events of March 1938 are too well known to bear repetition here; suffice it to say that Prüller, in his proud, black, SS uniform, returned with the Wehrmacht to Vienna, where he witnessed the frenzied, hysterical crowds welcoming the Germans, the *Anschluss* and Adolf Hitler.

The Nazis did not forget to reward their illegal Austrian party members. Prüller became a Vienna district office director of *Kraft durch Freude* (the Nazi organization for enabling their workers to have inexpensive holidays). He earned the respectable monthly sum of 350 Reichsmark; a chauffeured automobile was at his disposal. Now he could at last marry Henny—the pretty ash-blonde salesgirl of a department store on the Währingergürtel whom he had met one and a half years ago at the 'Ball of the Citizens of Hernals' (*Hernalser Bürgerball*).

Prüller and his bride had little time to enjoy peace and prosperity, however; for on 1st December 1938, Prüller was drafted into the German Wehrmacht. He was attached to the 6th Company of the 'Schützenregiment 10', a motorized battalion (U.S.: regiment) belonging to the Fourth Light Division, which in turn grew out of the old Austrian Second Field Regiment (U.S.: battalion), Feldjägerbataillon 2. After intensive training, the Division was made battle ready and, in the last golden days of August 1939, moved across Austria into Slovakia and took up a position on the Polish border.

S.L.
H.C.R.L.

Aachensee, July 1960

INDEX

INDEX

INDEX

INDEX